I0867256

ADVANCE PRAISE

"At INSIGNIA AUTO, we've seen firsthand how putting people at the centre transforms everything. By working together to help our team define and live their life plans - many for the very first time - we've given them a deeply personal gift that goes beyond the workplace. It reaches their families, their communities, and brings meaning to their everyday lives. The LET methodology - Logical, Emotional and Tactical - has been the key to making that transformation real. This book is packed with powerful yet practical insights any leader can apply. It's a must-read for those who want their organization to be more than just a place to work, but a space that leaves a lasting legacy in people's lives."

Gustavo Flores
Dealer Principal, INSIGNIA AUTO

Published by
LID Publishing
An imprint of LID Business Media Ltd.
LABS House, 15–19 Bloomsbury Way,
London, WC1A 2TH, UK

info@lidpublishing.com
www.lidpublishing.com

A member of:

BPR

businesspublishersroundtable.com

ISBN: 978-1-917391-37-5
ISBN: 978-1-917391-38-2 (ebook)

Cover and page design: Caroline Li

LET IT HAPPEN

How to deal successfully with change through LOGIC, EMOTION and TACTICS

MAU ESPINOSA

LID

MADRID | MEXICO CITY | LONDON
BUENOS AIRES | BOGOTA | SHANGHAI

CONTENTS

THE L.E.T. EFFECT

L.E.T. (Logic – Emotion – Tactics) is not just a framework, it's a philosophy of life and change, for both our personal and professional lives. This doctrine has been a guiding force throughout my life, even before I consciously identified it as such. It encapsulates how I have navigated significant decisions and events, balancing emotions, logic and tactical actions to achieve success.

From a young age, I applied these elements intuitively. Whether it was playing football (soccer), choosing my educational path or making a bold move to the US to advance professionally, I recognized the emotional underpinnings of these events. As you will see in the course of this book, understanding my own emotional landscape – knowing how it affected my decisions and actions – became crucial.

Logically, I realized that the education I received in college was a foundation, but not the entirety of what I needed in order to succeed. This awareness drove me to enhance my knowledge and skills whenever I had the opportunity. I pursued additional theoretical foundations, returning to school to study finance, economics and business valuation. I expanded my expertise through a negotiation program at Harvard Law School and earned a Master's degree in Leadership and Change from Oxford University and HEC Paris. It was there that I finally articulated the elements I had been practicing for years, and integrated them into my consulting services.

Since venturing into the world of consulting in 1996, initially as a financial analyst and eventually as the owner of my own firm, I have always understood the necessity of involving, empowering and providing emotional stability for people. This applies to individuals and small groups alike; without addressing group culture and people's emotions, sustainable change is impossible.

The process of change begins with emotions and is followed by logic. We must understand the 'why' and utilize available tools and resources to engage people and achieve results. The final piece is timing – prioritizing and making tactical moves, implementing changes, understanding the power of narrative (internal and external) and introducing new processes and tools.

Ultimately, this book aims to provide a comprehensive understanding of how to make decisions effectively. It emphasizes the importance of considering emotional implications, logical structures, processes, tools, resources, timing, prioritization, critical routes and all the other factors necessary for tactical decision making.

Integrating these elements will help you embrace the philosophy of L.E.T., allowing change to happen and fostering continuous growth and amazement in both your business and your personal life.

CHAPTER 1

A CALL TO LEAD

This is a book about change. Change in your personal life; change in your career; change in your business.

Dealing with change is the most important thing in our lives, whatever we're doing and at every stage. Nothing stays the same. We grow, we develop, we face setbacks and challenges. How we deal with those shifts in our lives and businesses determines whether we succeed or fail. I don't see change as a passive, external force. Rather, I see it as a **journey** that is purposeful, leadership-driven and empowering. This is a journey we must all lead for ourselves. It is my hope that this book will serve as an invitation to step into your role as a leader, not just in your professional life, but in your personal growth, as well.

Leadership is not a static state, it's a journey – a constant progression that requires logic, emotional strength and tactical precision. This book isn't just about understanding the process of transformation, it's about answering a call to lead through your personal and professional challenges.

Every journey starts with a spark: a moment of realization that the status quo is no longer enough. Whether you're navigating a new business challenge, overcoming personal setbacks or striving to improve your team's performance, the first step is always the same: recognizing that change is not optional, it's inevitable.

But this journey is not just about reaching an endpoint. It's about who you become along the way. Are you ready to take the wheel and lead yourself and others through the twists and turns of transformation?

THE JOURNEY DEFINED

The journey to lead begins with three interconnected dimensions: **Logic**, **Emotion** and **Tactics**. These three elements – L.E.T. – form the foundation of effective leadership and will help guide every step on the way.

1. **Logic**
   Your capacity for critical thinking, problem-solving and decision-making.

2. **Emotion**
   Your resilience, motivation and self-worth, which act as the fuel for the journey.

3. **Tactics**
   Your strategies, communication skills and adaptability, enabling you to navigate the unexpected.

Each dimension plays a vital role in shaping your path. However, as we'll explore, successful leaders often stumble when one of these elements is missing or misaligned.

We all know about logic. At every turn in our lives, we're faced with many issues. Our education has trained us to try to break issues down into their most significant constituent parts: as few as possible, and ideally two – a binary choice. We can do X or Y (or maybe Z). Which is likely to have the better outcome? We make a straightforward, logical decision based on those few alternatives and their expected outcomes. Logic gives us the confidence and a sense of security that the elements we took into consideration and the decisions we made were the correct ones. We feel we can look back on our decisions after the event and justify them by being able to demonstrate their logical foundations.

Except ... it doesn't always seem to work that way.

The logic may be impeccable, but we don't get the outcomes we expected.

Perhaps we know what we should do, but something seems to be holding us back. We don't actually carry through with the thing we know we ought to do, or perhaps others don't do what we think they ought to do, even though the logic seems clear and compelling. Our emotions, or the emotions of others, seem to be getting in the way.

Let's take a simple example, on a personal level. You decide to join a local gym. You feel you should be fitter and healthier. Maybe you could lose a couple of pounds. You might want to be stronger and in better shape. It's clear that's what you want, so you make a resolution to start working out. It's **logical**. It makes obvious sense that you should do this. You've thought about it, and this is the right course of action.

But when you get to the gym, it's difficult. You don't exercise as hard as you should, or for as long as you should. When it's time to go to the gym again, you put it off. It's tough to find the time, and you don't want to get up early, and work is really difficult just now, and the last time you went it made you stiff and sore. Your **emotions** are telling you that you aren't so keen on the whole workout thing, because it's not making you happy. In fact, it's downright painful. It's no fun.

So, then you apply some **tactics**. You hire a personal fitness trainer.

This first tactical decision makes a significant difference, but not just because someone is telling you what to do. The trainer doesn't just take your logical decision and force you to push through your emotional reluctance. Instead, based on their expertise and experience, they create a bridge between the two. The trainer works with your goals, breaks them down into short-term, achievable milestones, and designs a plan that lets you experience small, quick wins that build momentum.

For example, they don't just say, "Lose 20 pounds." Instead, they focus on smaller goals, like completing a consistent week of workouts, putting in a modest amount of time on the treadmill or lifting a certain weight. Bit by bit, these small successes help shift your narrative about fitness, turning it from a grueling obligation into a rewarding journey. The logical goal of getting healthier starts to feel emotionally fulfilling, because you see progress and begin to associate exercise with personal victories.

Additionally, your trainer helps you create a new vision for yourself. They encourage you to imagine how you'll look and feel six months from now – not just the physical changes, but the confidence and energy you'll carry. They paint a picture of that 'future you,' and, suddenly, the workouts are no longer just about today's discomfort; they're steps toward a vision that inspires you.

Perhaps most importantly, the trainer helps you build a routine that fits into your life. They work around your schedule, suggesting times that align with your natural energy levels and your day-to-day commitments. They even adapt exercises to fit what you enjoy, so the gym doesn't feel like a dreaded chore, but something you can embrace. This routine creates consistency, and consistency breeds habit.

In this way, hiring a trainer isn't just about having someone guide your workouts; it's the first tactical step in a series of strategic pivots. Short-term goals, a powerful vision and an adaptable routine are all tactics that bridge the gap between logic and emotion.

The logical strategy of getting healthier is correct, and your emotional reluctance isn't a weakness – it's a signal that something needs to change in how the strategy is being implemented. By using effective tactics, the tension between logic and emotion is resolved.

As simple as this solution may sound, in my work as a business consultant I see daily examples of incredible strategies that fail simply because the tactical steps to connect logic and emotion are overlooked. The key isn't just about having a great plan or the right mindset, it comes down to translating them into actionable, human-centered steps that work.

Let's look at another example. A lot of my experience has been as a consultant to automotive businesses. I've worked with car dealerships and service shops in the US, Mexico and Europe, dealing with multi-million-dollar operations that are often family businesses. It's different from the world of mega-corporations (though I have done consultancy work for those too). In many ways, it's more personal and more direct, which makes it more real. I've always loved that aspect of it.

In the auto service business, there is an issue with what is known as 'pro-efficiency.' This has to do with time available vs. time sold: a combination of productivity and efficiency. Productivity measures time worked vs. time available to work, while efficiency measures time sold vs. time worked. If you schedule two hours for a repair, for example, but you're able to complete the work in less than two hours, you bill the client for the time spent and move on to the next job. That is, of course, contingent on having repair jobs lined up in the pipeline. Otherwise, your mechanics will be sitting around with nothing to do. The ideal is to sell around 125% of available time, but most outlets average more like 80%.

There is a clear business **logic** that says you should aim to sell 125% of available service time. That gives a service manager a clear Key Performance Indicator (KPI) – a measure of progress toward a goal – which in this case is to achieve 125% pro-efficiency.

There's a real tendency for managers to announce, "OK, we have a new target. And the new target is to achieve 125% pro-efficiency. Yeah! Go team!" But to the team, that just sounds like more work. It comes across as an order to work harder. The compelling business logic is not so clear to them. Their **emotions** are not engaged.

But the increase in pro-efficiency – and in the business's productivity – could lead to the team earning as much as 60% more than they currently are. If the conversation with each individual team member begins with, "Hi John, how would you like to earn 60% more than you do at the moment?" the response is likely to be, "Just tell me what I need to do!" John is thinking about taking that money home to look after his family and do all the things he'd like to do if he had a bit more money to spend. Now his emotions are engaged. People don't necessarily need to know that the goal is to 'achieve 125% pro-efficiency.' What they do need to know is that management have found a way to potentially increase their pay by 60%. All the actions the management then take to show John and the rest of the team what they need to do – the various responsibilities, processes, dependencies and controls – are focused on them achieving a 60% increase in their pay, rather than on the manager's pro-efficiency target.

Presenting the logical goal in this **tactical** way has engaged emotions and massively increased the likelihood of business success.

I always say that the company's goal is just a milestone; a step along the way. The real goal, the one that truly drives action, is the executive's or individual's personal objective. This applies to sales, leadership, and every other aspect of business. The real goal isn't just selling X number of products, it's the commission the salesperson is chasing, the financial freedom they're striving for, the recognition they crave.

We need to shift the narrative around goal setting. It's not about abstract targets imposed from above; it's about connecting those targets to personal ambition. When individuals see their goals as deeply personal, when they understand the tangible rewards tied to their efforts, they don't just perform, they excel. That's how you build stronger, more consistent success. That's how you transform routine objectives into unstoppable momentum.

We're going to talk a lot more about L.E.T. – Logic, Emotion and Tactics – because I think you'll find it a wonderful tool for managing change in your life and in your business. It's a framework for understanding what's driving you, what's holding you back, and the various tactics that will help you link the logic to the emotions in every situation, and help you achieve your goals.

I'd like to share some examples of times in my own life when I was facing huge changes that threatened to inflict real damage on the things I had achieved, and show you the actions I took – based on logic, emotion and tactics – that allowed me to weather those storms, get back on track and make a success of my life.

Along the way, I'd also like to share some examples from my many years' experience as a consultant, working with businesses of all shapes and sizes to help fix real problems. I hope these will give you some useful, practical ideas about your own career, your own leadership or your own business.

But first, I'd like to provide a simple list of the things that experience has taught me are most important when it comes to getting things done in our personal and business lives: the ten most important motivators.

THE 10 PRINCIPAL MOTIVATORS:
LESSONS FROM MORE THAN 20 YEARS OF COACHING

In more than two decades of consulting, coaching and leading executive teams worldwide, I've learned that motivation isn't the same for everyone. Each person, from high-level executives to emerging leaders, is driven by unique factors that propel them to action. Unlocking motivation lies in understanding these fundamental drivers that fuel ambition, commitment and resilience.

For me, motivation is a word that combines 'motives' and 'action.' True motivation arises when we identify those underlying considerations that inspire purposeful action. When we deeply connect with what truly drives us, we align with our goals and achieve meaningful progress. These ten motivators are foundational, whether you're launching a small business, leading a multinational team or pursuing personal growth. We will refer back to these ten vital motivators many times in this book.

1. RECOGNITION

Recognition has a profound impact on people, extending far beyond celebrating visible successes. While recognizing achievements and results is vital, the true power of recognition emerges in difficult moments. Acknowledging when someone needs time to recover, when a team or individual faces complex challenges or when help is needed to overcome a barrier is even more valuable than spotlighting a win. This type of recognition conveys empathy, support and understanding, reinforcing trust and commitment.

2. COMPETITION

Healthy competition pushes individuals to surpass their perceived limits and reach greater heights. It fosters creativity, perseverance and continuous improvement. Leaders who tap into the spirit of competition know it can motivate people to innovate and perform at their best. Competition brings out qualities leaders need: resilience, determination and a hunger for excellence.

3. FREEDOM OF EXPRESSION

Having the freedom to express thoughts and ideas is incredibly powerful. This freedom creates a culture of respect and open dialogue, where team members feel safe challenging norms and exploring new solutions. When people feel heard, they engage more deeply, bringing powerful energy to every project because they know their voice matters.

4. GROWTH

Opportunities for growth are essential for any motivated professional. The absence of growth stifles motivation, while development renews it. Leaders who prioritize growth create environments where learning and development are encouraged. Growth provides people with a sense of progress and purpose, promoting continuous learning that not only enhances skills but also rekindles excitement and passion.

5. HAPPINESS (A POSITIVE ENVIRONMENT)

Creating a positive and supportive environment is crucial for fostering happiness and, consequently, inspiration. When leaders invest in a healthy workplace atmosphere, they create a foundation where people feel secure, supported and valued. Happiness at work promotes engagement and drives individuals to excel, creating a ripple effect that uplifts the entire team.

6. FINANCIAL REWARDS

While financial rewards alone don't guarantee sustained motivation, they provide essential security and a tangible measure of value. Compensation supports people's lives and enables them to pursue their goals and aspirations. Money can be a powerful incentive, especially when aligned with intrinsic motivators like purpose and recognition.

7. PURPOSE AND MEANING

Purpose gives meaning to work beyond profit and productivity. It's a powerful driver that inspires people to excel and persevere, even when times are tough. When people feel their efforts contribute to a larger mission, they gain satisfaction and clarity. Leaders who define and share purpose inspire their teams to work with dedication and vision, moving toward a common goal that is deeply fulfilling.

8. AUTONOMY AND CONTROL

Autonomy empowers individuals to make decisions and take responsibility for their roles. It is the freedom to act on their own judgement, fostering creativity, accountability and self-motivation. When leaders grant autonomy, they cultivate trust, demonstrating faith in their team's abilities. This trust transforms motivation into action, compelling people to make decisions with confidence and proactivity.

9. BELONGING AND CONNECTION

The need to belong and connect with others is fundamental. In a workplace context, feeling part of a team or community motivates people to go the extra mile. Leaders who foster a sense of belonging create strong bonds among team members, generating loyalty, trust and camaraderie. This sense of connection provides emotional support, making it easier to overcome challenges and celebrate successes together.

10. CHALLENGE AND MASTERY

Mastery is achieved by overcoming challenges and pushing personal boundaries. For many, the journey toward mastery is a powerful motivator. Leaders who introduce challenges encourage their teams to grow and excel, fostering a sense of accomplishment. By focusing on mastery, individuals develop resilience, confidence and an unstoppable drive to reach higher levels of competence, knowing that each step forward brings them closer to excellence.

CHAPTER 2

OXFORD

I was sitting in a pub in the university town of Oxford, England, in February 2020, drinking a beer with some fellow students.

Oxford is a long way from where I was born, in Querétaro, Mexico. Called the country's 'bellybutton' because of its central location, Querétaro is an historic city, the cradle of Mexican independence. Its famous aqueduct, built in the 18th century, towers over the city. The streets of the old city center are paved in pink cobbles. It is a place of romance and the ghosts of the past. If you close your eyes, you can still smell the horses that used to pull carriages through the city and hear the sound of their hooves on the cobbles.

The city is full of churches, their spires stretching up to the sky above the city streets wherever you look. When I was growing up there, it was a city of maybe half a million people, and I could bicycle from our home outside of downtown to my school on the other side of downtown in about ten minutes. The population of Querétaro has grown a lot in the last few decades. Many factors have caused this, including the high quality of life and the city's reputation as a good place to do business, but the general move of people away from Mexico City and into the interior of the country after the capital's devastating earthquake in 1985 was also a significant factor. My own father was a part of that story.

But on this day, I was not in Querétaro, Mexico, I was in Oxford, England, drinking English beer. English beer is hoppy and bitter and 'cellar cool,' which means warm to people from North America. But it grows on you. I got to like it. My favorite beers are ales and stouts. If you want to bring a smile to my face to this day, pour me a Guinness.

I was in my late 40s and studying for a Master's degree in Change Leadership. The course was split between Oxford University's Saïd Business School (named after Syrian/Canadian businessman and philanthropist Wafic Saïd) and the HEC business school in Paris (the École des Hautes Études Commerciales de Paris). I was learning a lot, which I discovered in my early years was very important for me and my future. My business back in the US and Mexico was doing well, though I'd had to rebuild it after the financial crash of 2008. More about that later.

The pub we were sitting in was older than the United States of America. The visible architecture dates back to at least the 1600s, but there has been a tavern and malthouse on the site since the 1300s. The pub is at the end of a narrow lane in the center of town, close to the ancient university colleges, libraries, theatres and churches that create Oxford's world-famous skyline. It was hard for me to believe I was sitting in a place where the great minds of the world had shared ideas, agreed and disagreed. Great scholars and writers like C.S. Lewis (*The Chronicles of Narnia*) and J.R.R. Tolkien (*The Lord of the Rings*). Famous philosophers like John Locke and Iris Murdoch. Famous playwrights like Oscar Wilde (*The Importance of Being Earnest*). Ground-breaking scientists like Stephen Hawking (the theory of black holes and *A Brief History of Time*). Actors like Hugh Grant (*Four Weddings and a Funeral* and *Bridget Jones's Diary*) and Rowan Atkinson (*Mr. Bean* and *Blackadder*).

And now, Mauricio Espinosa. Not famous, perhaps not destined for greatness, but studying here in the same place, trying to learn more about the world and put it to good use.

My thesis was due, and I and some fellow students had decided to rent an Airbnb just outside Oxford city as a kind of retreat. We were going to focus on getting our theses finished and doing nothing else (apart from the occasional trip to the pub). We would catch the bus into Oxford to use the library – the wonderful and beautiful Bodleian Library in central Oxford, which was founded in 1602 and is one of the oldest libraries in Europe. Who wouldn't want to study in a library like that? I spent many hours there, in awe of the simple fact that I was there, studying, where so many great minds had studied before me. I have a fascination with historic places. The fact that I am sharing an experience with so many of my fellow men and women who have passed this way before me fills me with emotion – just like the emotion I feel walking the cobbled street of Querétaro, surrounded by ghosts. My chest starts to feel heavy, and I find myself wiping away tears.

At the time I was studying in Oxford, Britain had been obsessed for many years with Brexit, the country's planned exit from the European Union, the political and economic partnership to which most European countries belonged. The country had voted to leave in a referendum in 2016, but the debate about how, and even if, to carry out Brexit had been raging in the British parliament and the nation ever since. The landslide election in December 2019 of a new UK Prime Minister, Boris Johnson, who had campaigned on a platform of 'Get Brexit Done,' meant that the great separation would finally happen. What would happen to the British economy and British society now that Brexit was a reality seemed like the big issue of the day. It took up most of our conversation in the pub that day.

And then, the first news started to trickle through about people in a place called Wuhan, in China, being taken ill with a pneumonia-like illness that reminded people of SARS (Severe Acute Respiratory Syndrome, or SARS-CoV-1). Suddenly, it seemed like a much bigger issue was bubbling up; something that might affect the whole world.

I had finished my thesis but still had my dissertation to write. I headed back home to Kansas City on March 10, 2020. I stopped over in Houston for a business meeting. The meeting was with a group that used to meet up two or three times a year, always in Houston. And because we are all creatures of habit, we tended to stay at the same hotel, eat at the same restaurant and do all the usual things in familiar places. The first thing I noticed was how quiet Houston's George Bush Intercontinental Airport was. The sprawling travel hub connects more than 170 cities worldwide, with 700 daily departures, handling some 40 million passengers annually, but it was almost deserted. So was the hotel. At the restaurant where we ate, the staff told us that, because of the spread of the pandemic, this was the last dinner they would serve before they closed the next day, with no idea when they'd reopen.

It was suddenly obvious to us all that this was serious. We rushed home and took COVID tests, worried about what we had been exposed to on our international flight, in the airport, at hotel and in the restaurant. The test results took 48 hours to come back. It was an anxious wait. Our tests were all negative, as it turned out, but we soon became aware of other people we knew who were testing positive. Those who did test positive felt almost ashamed, as if they had the plague or a sexual disease. People started to stay home to avoid contact with others. Businesses closed. People were frightened.

It reminded me of the financial crisis of 2008. Maybe it was worse. I'd almost lost my business then, and the way things were going I could lose it again. Right now. I had to act. Quickly.

The logic of the problem was obvious. My business was built around membership, like belonging to a gym. You pay a monthly fee, and you join a community of other businesses in your sector that gives you access to data on various key business measures, reflecting how everyone else in the community is performing. You can see how your company compares and share valuable information about best practices, common mistakes and anything else that might be helpful in improving your business.

I started out working for a company called NCM Associates, which developed the original '20 group' concept for the auto industry: creating a peer group of 20 auto dealers who would get together to benchmark and share best practices. Later, I had the opportunity to buy out the international division of that company and start my own business. More about that in the pages ahead.

Like I said earlier, I'd already had to rebuild that business once, following the 2008 crash and some complications in my personal life that I'll also tell you about later. Now, I stood to lose it all over again. Consultancy is an easy cost to cut. "Business is going to be terrible with this new COVID disaster, so I'll have to do without Mauricio. He's been great, and really helped my business, but first I have to survive."

So that was the clear logic of the situation. I faced a business meltdown because of the completely unexpected arrival of COVID.

Then there were the emotions involved. I knew that everyone was scared. I was scared myself. Scared on a personal level: would we get sick and die? And then, even if you hope you and your loved ones will survive, you start to wonder, "What about my customers in the auto business? What about their customers? Who's going to be buying cars? How can you run a business when people are frightened of meeting other people face to face? Will employees still come to work?"

I could see both the logic and the emotions. Now, I had to think about tactics.

When we are threatened and afraid, we need to move through various stages, as quickly as possible. After the first shock of fear and all the emotions that come with that – anger, uncertainty, anxiety and a search for answers – there are two options. You can succumb to the fear and say, "I don't know what to do. I've never experienced this before. I don't see how I can avoid disaster." Or, you can acknowledge the emotions you feel, understand them, and start to think creatively. When you're fearful, bad things – like the failure of your business – seem inevitable. You can't think what to do. But as you begin to acknowledge the situation and understand it better, you can begin to think creatively. You can start to believe that, maybe, some kind of success is a viable alternative. And then you can move into a growth phase, where you set new, achievable goals with a clear vision. A phase where actions take place. And when you combine action with vision, you start to execute properly again; you feel real belief in the possibility of success.

Back on that Sunday in March of 2020, I was thinking about the threat that logic told me we were all about to face, about the emotions we were all going through – my own emotions included – and about a tactical response that could help me save my business.

Looking back, I see now that Oxford was more to me than a moment in time. It became a mirror, reflecting who I was, what I aspired to be, and what I needed to change in order to align those two realities. It wasn't just about acquiring knowledge or credentials, but gaining clarity and conviction. The walls of that historic institution carried the echoes of great thinkers, and, in that space, I discovered that leadership, at its core, is deeply personal.

This journey wasn't simply about learning frameworks or theories. It was about unearthing my own capacity to lead, starting with leading myself. The experiences, the people and the profound challenges I faced pushed me to ask hard questions: **What do I stand for? What legacy do I want to leave? How do I build something enduring, not just for others, but for myself?**

Through this process, I found inspiration – not in external accolades or expectations, but in the quiet confidence that comes from knowing yourself. The ability to define success on your own terms is a freedom few pursue, yet it is essential for true leadership.

As I step, yet again, into a new phase of life, Oxford reminds me of a crucial truth: leadership isn't about perfection or certainty. It's about growth. It's about the courage to start, the humility to learn and the resilience to adapt. This new phase is my next great journey, not just as a professional, but as a leader who seeks to inspire and uplift others.

Oxford was the catalyst, but the road ahead is where the real work begins. And I am ready.

CHAPTER 3

COVID

In 2020, with COVID spreading and my business at risk of collapse, I decided to send a message to every one of my clients. I hoped it would be a powerful message, giving them the opportunity to participate in a weekly or even a daily forum, to talk about what was happening in their personal lives and in their businesses in this new era of disruption and uncertainty.

My first goal was to move everybody out of fear and into an acknowledgement that this bad thing was happening. The sooner we could face the facts, the faster we could start creating solutions.

My own fear, of course, was that my clients would simply stop their membership. I might retain some of them on a fee basis, but that would undercut my whole business model. My goal was to retain 70% of my client base. As it turned out, I held onto 96% of them. I lost just three through the whole of COVID, out of the 70 clients I'd had at the time. I attribute that to the first message I sent them on that Sunday, March 22. The day after my birthday. My 51st birthday was the day of L.E.T. – Logic, Emotion and Tactics. A day I will never forget.

I wrote out the message I planned to send to my clients, but the more I read it, the more I realized that a written message was not going to cut it. When you read something, you don't receive the emotion that lies behind that message. It can seem too businesslike, as if it's nothing out of the ordinary and no big deal. Or, if you're going through high emotion yourself, your own emotions color what you're reading, and the message can seem inappropriate or misspoken. I needed people to see my face, hear my voice and be able to understand my own emotions. I decided to go with a video message. I must have shot the video a half-dozen times and made various edits before I finally thought, "This is the one."

It was probably one of the first COVID-related messages they got, because I sent it on that Sunday. I didn't wait for Monday morning and opted against a group message – I sent the messages on Sunday night, individually, via WhatsApp, to every one of my clients. That was a tactical decision. I could have made it easier for myself and created a distribution list. One click: there you go! But the fact that they saw it coming directly to them made it personal. Many clients have told me since that time that the one-on-one correspondence was important to them. "Hey, Mau, you reached out to me directly, on a Sunday, telling me that it was going to be OK, and that you were going to be there with me. And the first thing you were going to do was to have a meeting the next morning, with everybody who could make it. And that gave me reassurance."

I actually called the first sessions with this new group 'vomit sessions,' because I invited people to just let all their bad feelings out. People were in literal survival mode, worrying about how to move money and whether money would even be worth anything, and how they could buy essential things, just to get by day-to-day. Everyone was in a very dark place.

The early news about the pandemic was very depressing; very bad. People started to die. From zero COVID fatalities in March 2020, the US had 100,000 deaths by the end of May. Mexico had reached around 20,000 deaths. There was this new and constant threat, but people started to adjust. They immediately took measures for their own personal safety, and then they began to think about how to deal with this new reality.

I sent notes and articles to the group every day. Beyond talking about COVID in general, I engaged with them on what was happening with their own situation. I started to apply everything I'd learned about change in my Master's program, which had prepared me for precisely this moment. All I could think was: "This is VUCA!" – the concept of Volatility, Uncertainty, Complexity and Ambiguity. In my mind, I could hear my wonderful professors explaining the concepts, and feel how the knowledge I had just acquired was ready to be used in practice. All of the messages, articles and notes that I wrote or forwarded had a distinct theme of *change*.

"Be careful," I told the group. "Everybody's scared. Everybody's looking for answers, but there are no answers right now. You're going to find whatever you want to find, and a lot that you don't want to see, on the internet. You want to find out how many people are going to die? There are going to be a lot of people who will tell you that everybody's going to die. Stop searching."

That was my first advice to the group: stop *doom-scrolling* online. Start working with what you have. What can we do? Can we keep part of our revenue? How can we talk to our clients? Many people will decide to keep their old car while the future is so uncertain, but those cars are going to need maintenance. Some people will find that their whole lifestyle has changed, so maybe they need a different kind of vehicle. We started working through that – acknowledging the situation, assessing our options, understanding what services we could provide. Many truly valuable ideas were shared in those early weekly meetings.

After about 15 days, people began to move from fear and reaction to acknowledgement and creativity, to talking about possible solutions. "What if we do this?" "How about if we do that?" "I'm gonna try this at my company." "Oh, that's a great idea, but what if we ..."

In the groups, I started hearing all these ideas and solutions, and you could see the beginnings of a change in people's emotions from fear to understanding – the first step in dealing with fear. Then, at the end of the first month, we started to look at the numbers in people's individual businesses. A lot of them were not as bad as everyone had expected. Two months later, they were still not as bad as expected. It seemed people's worst fears were unfounded.

At this point, everyone could begin to think logically again. They had been afraid of losing 90% of their revenue, or of seeing it plummet to zero – just as I had. Now, we were beginning to see that people had lost maybe 50% or less of the revenue. Most businesses had adjusted salaries, trying to keep people employed with a temporary reduction in pay, and had put other essential cost-saving measures in place. There was now real hope that everyone could get through this and emerge safe and sound on the other side. (It's worth adding that Mexico was one of the countries that did not provide governmental aid to businesses or individuals. It's also the case that the longer-term economic benefit of government-funded programs in those countries that did provide state aid is still up for discussion. Such programs were certainly inflationary.)

People's emotions were changing. We had spent the first month or two moving from fear to acknowledgement to creativity, and from there we could begin to think about growth.

We started working on the phases of change. The first step in any change process is to develop a clear vision that will act as a roadmap to future success. I started to craft a narrative about vision with the group, something we really needed at the time. I didn't call it 'vision' at that point, because when things are difficult people tend to think they need immediate fixes rather than a longer-term vision. The leader needs to have a vision of how we will emerge from this process of change, because dealing with an immediate threat is still a process of change, and if we don't treat it as such we're simply reacting in the moment without any coherent plan. But the leader doesn't have to *present* it as a vision. Different words may resonate better with people in these circumstances. Also, 'vision' doesn't only mean long-term vision; in this case, we needed short-term vision. The narrative became, "Let's get this week done. Let's have some actions to focus on and then let's discuss our results next Monday."

One of my core principles in business is that **vision plus narrative equals perseverance.** Decide on your vision and build a narrative around it. That will give you the perseverance that will help you achieve your vision. One week was all I was asking for, to at least begin to move toward the realization of our short-term vision. Allow one week of creativity and small actions. And, like magic, emotions started to shift.

In our group sessions, I opened with, "OK, guys. We've been through the last couple of months, and we're still here. We're all still operating. Now, let's start looking a little bit further ahead. How's your business going to look in a few months' time? Or a year from now?" And I started planting the seed of a longer-term vision in each of them, and how we were going to create that, and how we were going to communicate it. I started to ask who in their organization was going to be able to help with the process of change. Who would be the agents of change, which I call 'drivers' of change? Who would be the driver in this department, or in that area? Let's say one of our participants had seven car dealerships, for example. How many drivers of change did they have in each of those locations? People who would help you achieve what you need, because you can't do it on your own? These don't have to be people who are currently in positions of management. Any team member can help drive change. Sometimes, somebody closer to the action can be a more effective leader for change than one who has 'manager' in their job title.

I was trying to help clients think in terms of creating a reimagined leadership team to help them achieve their vision. Who the best people were to help them lead this process of change and how these leaders were going to do it in practice; what meetings they should have and what the agenda should be; how they were going to help people with working from home; how to deal with all the practical issues that came with running a business during the pandemic.

All of these actions stemmed from the moment I touched down at Houston's airport, saw that it was nearly deserted, and realized that my business and all my clients' businesses were facing a monumental crisis.

I had about 70 clients at the time, but soon we started having 300 or 400 people through the course of a week join our Zoom meetings, because I'd sent an invitation to all my past clients and everybody I had in my database. I wanted to offer a service to help us all pull through this; it wasn't exclusively for my current clients. (Later, it did become an exclusive program for my clients.)

We started benchmarking best practices, which was at the heart of what my business did. We could say, "Hey, this is working well in these three cities; let's look carefully at what they're doing there." And all of a sudden, we started seeing creativity.

Around this time, total weekly attendance of the meetings started going down. People began to feel more comfortable, and think they didn't need this group meeting anymore, which is an emotional reaction. You feel safer, more secure, so you feel you don't need the support network any longer. But tactical thinking would remind you that this process, these meetings, are what have brought you back to this safe place, so maybe you should keep joining the meetings.

At the end of the crisis, probably 3% of my clients ended up with overall losses, while everybody else kept decent profits. And I kept 67 of my 70 clients. My total number of clients has roughly tripled since then.

That one decision, on Sunday, March 22, 2020, was driven by emotion – the fear of losing my business. It was supported by logic – you've been here before, after the 2008 financial crash, and turned possible failure into success by tactics – the decision to send a personal message to every one of my clients right then and there, while the issue was at the top of everyone's minds, inviting them to join a business support group to help everyone get through the coming crisis.

Today, I look back on that episode as the key, defining moment in my business career. Surviving the 2008 crash was a big deal, but it felt more 'normal.' Economies go through cycles and sometimes nose-dive; the Great Recession after the 2008 crash was exceptional, but not unprecedented. COVID felt different. It took the whole world by surprise, and we didn't have any meaningful precedent to guide us. The Spanish Flu epidemic of 1918–1920, which broke out in the final stages of the First World War, was the previous deadliest pandemic, killing an estimated 25–50 million people worldwide, but it had faded from human memory. The awful death toll tended to merge, in terms of history, with that of the war itself (an estimated 15–22 million military personnel and civilians). Before that, there was the Black Death of the 14th century, which wiped out roughly half the population of Europe, but was so far back in history that it has become meaningless to most people, except perhaps as an atavistic fear that we really were going back to the Dark Ages.

But now, through it all, here we are. We have survived! There were around seven million deaths worldwide attributed to COVID-19. The more remarkable figure is that nearly seven million more people contracted the virus but survived.

The main lesson I took from the pandemic was so profound for me that I rewrote my dissertation for my Master's degree. I had already submitted my thesis on Change Leadership, but my dissertation was not yet due. I felt the need to change the conclusion to reflect what I felt I had learned from this episode in my life. Something about the seriousness of the crisis – the fact that we were talking about the survival of people's businesses and livelihoods, let alone their actual physical survival – brought home forcefully to me that, at heart, we work for our own lives and the things that matter to us personally. We don't work 'for' a company. We work *at* the company, but we work for our own personal benefit. That's a big change in mindset. I work *at* this company, but I work *for* myself because I have this vision in my life, I have this purpose in my life, and the financial income I need to be happy comes from here. People work for the benefit of their lives. I built this realization into what I call a **Life Plan** that I still use when I give people advice about their personal lives and their personal finances. I make sure they understand that we all work for our own lives.

For a business owner, of course, it's different. The business is their financial input and their life's work and the thing that supports their family. Everything they care about is wrapped up in the business. But if I work at the company, even as a director, it's still a transactional relationship. That *quid pro quo* might be so favorable that it feels like an enduring commitment. But even the best-paid, most committed director might one day walk away because the company isn't giving them something they need for themselves: personal growth; a sense of achieving something more meaningful and important in their lives; more personal time for themselves and their families. They work *at* the company, but they work *for* themselves.

We need to remind ourselves of this fundamental fact when we deal with our colleagues and employees – the people who make our businesses run. They will only wholeheartedly do things that they understand are genuinely in their best interest. They may pay lip service to a program of change, but if they don't understand in their hearts that this change will bring some real benefit to them, they'll never be wholeheartedly behind it because their emotions are not engaged.

I'd like to finish this chapter with a reflection on where we are today. We have come through COVID and, in the USA and in Mexico at least, the economy is getting better. Businesses are making money. People have cash in their pockets, so there is less urgency for change. When COVID hit, the gravity of the situation was inescapable. People felt it in their guts. It was a threat to their livelihoods and their whole way of life.

It's a lot easier to feel a sense of urgency when there is an obvious threat. When there is no immediate threat, we feel happy. We're complacent. Our emotions tell us that everything is fine: there's nothing to worry about and we can relax. But change is still happening, whether we notice it, or like it or not. In reality, post-COVID, people's attitudes toward work are changing quite radically.

More change is coming our way. The economy is up now, but it will turn down again one day soon. If we're at the top of that curve right now, we need to create an even better vision, a desire to keep this success and to keep growing and to be agile in the face of the changes we can already see coming our way. Today, the world finds itself once again confronting widespread disruption and uncertainty. Global leaders' decisions are creating powerful ripples, some embraced enthusiastically by their supporters, others fiercely contested. Tariffs reshaping international trade; the prolonged and turbulent conflict between Russia and Ukraine, unsettling global stability and impacting energy prices and global supply chains; debates around NATO's relevance and future, and the unpredictable impact of AI – all these illustrate how swiftly our collective reality can shift. Much like COVID, these events challenge our resilience, demand rapid adaptability, and test the credibility of leadership. We must remind ourselves that disruption, whether driven by nature, politics, or innovation, continuously reshapes our world. The skills honed during the pandemic – adaptive leadership, agile decision-making and deep emotional intelligence – remain vital as we navigate this latest turbulence. Our journey through COVID taught us that surviving disruption is not merely about weathering the storm but about emerging stronger, more prepared and more deeply connected than before.

Change is the one constant of business. The most important task of any leader when times seem good is to make change happen *now*, ahead of the curve, so that the business is prepared for the changes coming its way. Otherwise, we will find ourselves again in the place we were when COVID struck, fighting a battle for which we had not prepared.

Looking back at the early days of the pandemic, I remember the overwhelming uncertainty, not just in my professional life but in every aspect of existence. The world changed overnight, and so did the rules. As I sat at my desk, staring out at the rapidly shifting landscape, I realized this was no ordinary challenge. This was a test of adaptability, resilience and belief in oneself.

The truth is, I didn't have all the answers. None of us did. But what I did know was that self-credibility – believing in myself first

– would be my foundation. You see, credibility isn't just about how others perceive you and having every solution at hand. It begins closer to home, with confidence in your own attributes and capabilities, the courage to admit what you don't know, the humility to learn and the determination to act decisively.

During those early days, I discovered the power of agility. Decisions that once took weeks needed to be made in hours. Plans that were carefully crafted were suddenly obsolete. It was like steering a ship in a storm, with the waves of uncertainty crashing from every direction. But adaptability isn't just about surviving the storm. It's about finding a way to thrive in it.

I turned to the concept of adaptive leadership, the model developed by Harvard professors Ronald Heifetz and Marty Linsky. It's something I'd encountered before as a concept, but never truly lived until this moment. Heifetz and Linsky's idea of distinguishing technical problems from adaptive challenges resonated with me. This wasn't a time for routine fixes or waiting for things to go back to normal. It was a time to experiment, to learn and to pivot.

And pivot we did. I remember working with a client who was paralyzed by the chaos. Their business, built on decades of tradition, suddenly had to embrace online sales and remote work. At first, there was resistance – fear of change, uncertainty about the unknown. But through collaboration, transparency and small, actionable steps, we turned their hesitation into momentum. It wasn't easy, but it was transformational.

As I've said, I learned during this time that credibility isn't just what others see in you. It's rooted in what you see in yourself. It's waking up every morning, even in the face of fear, and choosing to trust your instincts, your preparation and your ability to figure things out. Credibility grows when you embrace adaptability, not as a buzzword, but as a way of being.

COVID didn't just teach me to adapt, it reminded me that agility and credibility are deeply intertwined. When you're agile, you're open to change. When you're credible, others trust you to lead them through it. Together, they form the essence of leadership in times of crisis and beyond.

As the storm of the pandemic began to calm, I realized that the lessons learned weren't just for that moment. They were for life. Adaptability isn't something we switch on during emergencies, it's a muscle we must strengthen every day. And credibility? It starts with believing in yourself, so others can believe in you too.

I share this because we all face our own storms, whether it's a global pandemic, a personal challenge or a professional setback. The question isn't whether the storms will come – they will. The question is how we'll navigate them.

For me, the answer lies in adapting quickly, staying grounded in self-belief and building the kind of trust that inspires others to follow. That's how we move forward, no matter how daunting the journey ahead may seem.

CHAPTER 4

RESILIENCE

This seems like a good point to share some thoughts about resilience.

Resilience is not an innate trait. It is cultivated through life's trials, learning, growth and intentional strategies. It is the ability to adapt to stressors and maintain psychological wellbeing in the face of adversity, allowing us to bounce back from challenges. Adversity itself takes many forms. Sometimes it strikes like lightning – visible, urgent and demanding immediate action, as with the global wave of COVID-19. Other times it arrives quietly, almost imperceptibly at first, whispering that it is on our doorstep. A business gradually loses traction, relationships weaken or personal habits erode success, and yet, we fail to recognize the growing threat until it feels insurmountable.

Let's explore resilience from a two-dimensional perspective, where threats, whether loud or silent, shape our emotional and behavioral responses across three stages: Uncertainty, Recognition and Growth.

DIMENSION 1: URGENT ADVERSITY – THE COVID WAVE

When COVID hit, it was a storm no one could ignore. Offices closed overnight, routines vanished and fear took hold. The urgency of the situation forced individuals and organizations to react immediately.

- **UNCERTAINTY – REACTION**

The sudden onset of the crisis triggered anger, uncertainty and anxiety. Leaders desperately sought answers, but the noise of the unknown made clarity elusive. People clung to excuses: "It's temporary." "We'll get through it." "It's out of our control." Failure seemed likely; almost inevitable.

- **RECOGNITION – CREATION**

As the initial impact subsided, some began to see opportunities amid the chaos. With empathy and creative problem-solving, businesses reinvented themselves. Remote work was implemented, online services expanded and communities rallied together. Success started to feel possible.

- **GROWTH – ACTION**

The most resilient leaders didn't just adapt, they thrived. They set clear goals and collaborated on new strategies, transforming fear into opportunity. Decisive action proved that resilience could turn an existential threat into a platform for innovation.

DIMENSION 2: SILENT ADVERSITY – THE WHISPERING THREAT

In contrast, there is a subtler form of adversity: slow erosion. Imagine managers becoming more stressed, team morale declining and small but consistent drops in performance. A business owner notices minor decreases – slightly fewer showroom visits or delayed orders – but dismisses them as temporary, citing a strong market. Over time, profitability dwindles. Months later, the crisis feels urgent, but it has been taking root silently, and going unaddressed, for weeks or months.

- **UNCERTAINTY – REACTION**

Realization comes late, accompanied by doubt, anger and anxiety. The business owner might say, "We've overcome this sort of thing before," or blame external factors, like the government or market conditions. But when the crisis feels real, fear paralyzes action.

- **RECOGNITION – CREATION**

Some leaders recognize early signs and adopt a mindset of awareness. They analyze feedback, seek external opinions and approach the situation with curiosity and creativity. Meetings with their people, participation in professional networks like G20, and consistent communication of a clear vision foster optimism and a viable path forward.

- **GROWTH – ACTION**

Leaders who act early regain control. They pivot strategies, invest in their teams, and communicate a compelling vision. With clear direction and measurable steps, they create an upward spiral of resilience that reverses the decline.

A CYCLE OF RESILIENCE: FROM FEAR TO GROWTH

Both urgent and silent threats highlight a universal truth: resilience is a dynamic process. It is not linear, and falling back into fear is natural. Leaders who cultivate awareness, creativity and collaboration foster a positive cycle between Recognition and Growth, reducing the risk of slipping back into fear.

KEY LEADERSHIP LESSONS IN RESILIENCE

1. STAY ALERT TO SILENT THREATS

Resilience begins with awareness. Pay attention to small changes in behavior, performance or relationships before they escalate. Recognize signs of anxiety or uncertainty within your team – they often indicate fear.

2. EMBRACE CREATIVITY AS A PATH TO ACTION

When fear strikes, shift focus toward possibilities. Collaboration and brainstorming can transform uncertainty into opportunity. Host creative thinking workshops or seek professional support from networks like G20 to explore innovative solutions.

3. COMMIT TO CONSISTENT GROWTH

Growth is not a destination but a series of actions rooted in clear goals, trust and execution. Resilient leaders inspire their teams to move forward one step at a time. Short-term goals build credibility and provide the flexibility to adapt and adjust.

A TALE OF TWO BUSINESSES

Two friends ran competing car dealerships. When COVID struck, both faced the same challenges: closures, reduced customer traffic and an uncertain future. One waited for things to get better, making excuses and letting time pass. The other took action. He joined his G20 network, shared ideas, received feedback and adapted his business model.

The difference was clear: one survived and thrived, while the other failed to overcome adversity. The key was not just action, but resilience and the power of belonging to a G20 network, where the phases of adversity – Uncertainty, Recognition and Growth – were transformed into steps toward success.

Resilience is a learned skill developed through the phases of Uncertainty, Recognition, and Growth. Leaders play a critical role in navigating these phases, fostering emotional awareness, strategic behavior and sustainable growth.

CHAPTER 5

NOT BEING PELÉ

I'd like to tell you a bit more about my life, because it has, of course, shaped the way I am, the way I think and all the ideas I'm sharing here.

When I was growing up in Querétaro, my nickname was Pelé, like the famous football player. But it wasn't because I was a great football player.

I wasn't a bad player. I was just a regular teenage player who liked to be on the team, and I was good enough to make the team, but that was it. But I was given the nickname of the best player in the world. And that had more to do with my skin color than my football skills, so that was unsettling. It created emotional challenges in my mind, because I knew how I got the nickname. It wasn't recognizing any talent I had or celebrating who I was as a person, it was about something I couldn't do anything about: the way I looked. And because kids are cruel, maybe there was some mockery in calling me Pelé, arguably the greatest player of all time and a really good-looking guy, when I wasn't anything special at football and I didn't think I was good looking. It didn't feel like an affectionate nickname; it felt cruel.

There were some other, more significant challenges for me as I was growing up. My cousin, who was also my best friend, died in a plane crash when I was ten years old. That hit me very hard. You understand that older people die, but as a child you don't expect your friends to die. Then, when I was 15, someone who had become important to me as a mentor also died in a tragic accident. And then I lost another great friend when I was just about to start college. That's a lot of deaths for a young person to handle. It made me question whether entering into loving and caring relationships was too dangerous, and it would be safer to build an emotional shield around myself and keep my distance from people, to avoid the risk of future loss and pain.

I wasn't a brilliant student. I was a smart person, but I wasn't a brilliant student. I knew I could get by with the grades I could get and that would be good enough, because that was the expectation

I felt people had of me. You just have to be good enough. That's it. You don't need to be excellent. Just be good enough, and that will see you through. The attitude seemed to be, "The kid's not a great student and he hasn't got the looks, but he'll be fine. He'll do OK." That was the label I felt I had: that nobody expected too much of me. I was angry and upset with life, and I became something of a rebel. I got into a lot of trouble. I climbed Querétaro's famous aqueduct on a dare and got into trouble with the authorities. It is alleged that I snuck back into my school one night to change an examination paper I knew I had flunked, but that's not true. I did get into a lot of fights. They were usually fights I had no reason to be involved in, but I would find myself in the middle of them, usually because I felt the need to support somebody who was being attacked. I was always a good friend to people who were kind to me; I found myself to be very loyal to kindness. To this day, I find my nephews and nieces have stories they heard about me and my exploits growing up in Querétaro.

When I was a teenager, bullfights were a big part of city life in Querétaro. The bullfighting season was a highlight of the year, with weekends dedicated to dressing up and gathering at the Plaza de Toros. I remember attending the *corridas*, where the spectacle involved six bulls and three different *toreros*.

In the Spanish tradition, bullfighting is not literally a fight; it is more of a dramatic dance between man and bull, even though the drama culminates in the killing of the animal. Each *torero* would face off against two bulls, creating a series of intense, emotional encounters. Within the bullfighting world, there are different styles: the traditional *toreros* or *matadores* perform on foot, with the *rejoneadores* engaging in the dance on horseback, often changing horses multiple times during the performance.

But there is another traditional type of *torero*, the *forcados*, which originated in Portugal. And this is where my story takes a turn.

In the realm of bullfighting, *forcados* are a traditional team of bullfighters who perform in a Portuguese style known as *pega de cara*, or 'face catch.' Unlike the matadors, who use capes and swords, the *forcados* confront the bull bare-handed and unarmed. A typical group consists of eight members who work together to subdue the bull in a series of coordinated actions. In the bullfights in Querétaro, the *forcados* were like an extra piece of entertainment. The *rejoneador* would go off for a change of horse, and the *forcados* would come on to entertain the crowd, engaging the bull with our bare hands.

The tradition is a celebrated part Portuguese cultural heritage. Whereas in Portugal the *caveileros*, who fought the bull on horseback, were typically from the aristocratic classes, the *forcados* were from working-class backgrounds, forming amateur associations. In Querétaro, a group called the *Forcados Querétanos*, founded in 1986, became renowned for their skill, bravery and dedication to the art of *pega de cara*. Some of my cousins and their friends were the originators of this group. One cousin was a *matador*, another a *rejoneador*, from the Spanish school of bullfighting, and they were an inspiration to the circle.

My friends and I decided to form our own group. We trained and sought opportunities to prove ourselves. We took part in small festivals, eventually catching the attention of the main group. They started to train and guide us, and some of our members eventually joined their ranks.

In *pega de cara*, the team forms a line, facing the bull, and the bull can only see this as a shape. It doesn't know the shape is a line of people. The frontman in the line provokes the bull into charging at him, then steps aside at the last moment. The second in line grabs the bull by the horns, or round the neck, and tries to hold it while the rest of the team pile on, with one person grabbing its tail, to try to subdue and halt the animal.

I was usually second in line, which is the most dangerous position. You cannot see the bull until the last moment, when the first in line, who had provoked it into charging, steps aside and lets you get to work. There's a high risk of getting gored or trampled if you don't get a very firm grip on the bull in the first seconds. It takes a lot of strength and a lot of courage. Or, you could argue, a lot of stupidity.

After the *forcados* have done their work and entertained the crowd, the *rejoneador* comes back into the arena on a fresh horse, and then the *matador* enters the arena, and the complex dance between man and bull continues to its dramatic climax.

During my junior and senior years of high school, I had three dreams in life, in this order: to be an actor, a footballer or a bullfighter. None of them materialized. I'm not sure if I lacked the talent or simply a concrete plan. Sometimes I think, "I could have been a good actor," but I never took part in school plays or pursued acting seriously. Football was similar; despite playing in high school and college, I felt I lacked the talent to go further. As for the *forcados* ... well, it was a bad idea from the start. I did it to fit in, to be noticed, not because it was a genuine passion. In reality, I don't enjoy bullfights or all the surrounding glamor and excitement.

We all have moments when we need to stop and assess our situations. Is this really what I want? If so, what am I doing to make it happen? If I'm struggling, is the struggle physical or emotional? Am I genuinely struggling to achieve this thing, or is there something emotional holding me back: some lack of commitment?

I don't regret any of it because it gave me the perspectives I use today to analyze my life and understand patterns: what caused certain behaviors, and how I reacted. It taught me how much emotion influenced my decisions, and how absent logic and tactics were at that time.

When my mother found out about my involvement with my cousins and friends in the *forcados*, she was horrified. You know how mothers are, always imagining that something bad will happen – and in this case, that meant me being maimed or killed. But she also thought, as a mother would, that I was being influenced for the worse by the people I'd fallen in with – by my cousins and my wider circle of friends and the *Forcados Querétanos*.

She and my father decided to take me out of that environment. I had finished high school, and their solution was simple but life-changing: they sent me to stay with an American family they had connections with. The family lived in a place called Protection, in Comanche County, Kansas. It was a small, rural town with a population of maybe 600 people.

Back then, Protection didn't even appear on Google Maps. It had one bar, two cafes and a gas station. But for me, it was a place that changed my life – a testament to the importance of understanding our motivations and the decisions that shape our lives. It's about finding clarity amid chaos and learning to navigate the dance of life with purpose and passion.

I didn't speak any English when I arrived with my new family. I knew three words: 'yes,' 'no' and 'maybe.' Those were my only words for at least my first ten days. People were very kind to me, and would speak to me very slowly, and I would experiment with my three-word vocabulary and try to understand what the question had been from what people's reactions to my answers were.

My best friend to this day is from Protection. He was the one who basically taught me how to speak English. We communicated in signs and sounds. He would say, "Let's play a video game," and make bleeping sounds – the kind of noises and music you get in video games – and I would understand. And he'd say, "Video game" again, and I would link the sounds of the words to the meaning, and we would move on from there. His name was Mike, and I still tell him that he is responsible for my English. "Good or bad, buddy, it's yours. How I speak English is down to you!"

I started making new friends and discovering a different kind of people. Midwesterners tend to see the good in people. They can be very conservative in their political views, but they really want to live a life of love and happiness, and they embraced me in their society. It was a different world – a world of around 600 people, vs. half a million people in the city where I grew up. All of a sudden, everything was different. For whatever reason, people were far more supportive. They were saying, "Oh, you're great! You're a great sportsman. A wonderful person!" The narrative started to change, which was a cultural thing, a difference between the American way of thinking and how life was at home in Mexico.

My parents' plan had been that I would stay in Protection for the summer and then go back to Querétaro. But my new family said they could get me a place in the local high school for my senior year, and I was enjoying myself and the fact that my English was improving day by day. They liked having me there, and asked my parents if I could maybe stay for another year. They agreed, and I did a final year of high school in Protection.

That change of narrative in my life at that age gave rise to an emotion I hadn't experienced before: self-esteem. It created a real desire to be successful. A desire to go back home and show everyone what I could be – that I could be more than what everybody was thinking I could be.

I went back home to Querétaro believing in myself. I was a different kid.

As I was finishing high school in Protection, I had begun to discover that I was really quite a smart person. I was able to not just come out of college as the top student in my class, but also as a very resourceful person. I started learning how to talk in public and to give speeches. I started to learn how to debate. I started learning how to inspire people. I started learning how important it was to have positive people around me, and that the only way to have positive people around me was to become positive in my own outlook on life.

I started studying people. I started studying people in history and different characters, some of them fictional. I still say to my friends that my personality has been built around three fictional characters and one non-fiction character. The fictional characters were James Bond, Bruce Wayne and Sherlock Holmes. The real-life character I always found inspiring was Albert Einstein. Not so much because he was the greatest mind in the world, but because I wanted to know how he became the greatest mind in the world; how he achieved that in his life.

I loved James Bond because he was so resourceful. His enemies would have him pinned down, but he would find something – maybe one of his clever gadgets from Q – to get him out of the fix he was in. I loved how Sherlock Holmes would look at every detail in the cases he was faced with and see that the answers were always in front of you; you just had to look for them. That's a very tactical approach. Start by looking at what's right in front of you, almost hitting you in the face, because that probably holds the answer to what you are looking for.

And then there was Bruce Wayne. What I loved about him was that he was Bruce Wayne, he was not Batman. Batman was like a character he played, a persona he took on. There was a lot I liked about Batman, but there was more I liked about Bruce Wayne, who saw his parents murdered when he was a child and swore a vendetta of justice against criminals. I hadn't lost my parents, but I had lost a lot of people who were very important to me. It was not easy. I think that was why I related especially to Bruce Wayne, who carried around this burden of sadness and anger about the deaths of his parents, and who fought back against criminals like I had fought back against the bullies in the schoolyard in Querétaro.

Other than these important people in my life that I'd lost, my circle of friends when I was younger had been quite bullying. I don't mean that they made my life a misery all the time, but that was the nature of the relationship between us. This meant that I was always the butt of jokes, always having to play the part, always putting up with something unpleasant.

You feel the need to be part of a group at that age, and you start maybe accepting that all this bullying is part of who you are and what you have to endure. Later on in life, you realize it doesn't have to be that way. That's why those relationships completely disappeared from my life when I started looking at things in a more logical way and deciding, "No. I'm not going to hang out with this crowd. I'm going to hang with people who are positive toward me, and think well of me, and don't get their kicks from trying to put me down and make fun of me."

That created the emotion that helped me on the next part of my journey. I guess a lot of teenagers go through something similar, but I decided I had to overcome that kind of limiting view of what I could achieve with my life. I was feeling a lot of emotion, quite a lot of pain, but I started to become very logical about things. I thought to myself: How can you get around this? How can you be successful? How can you create a better life for yourself? That took me into thinking, Well, if I have these weaknesses, then I should find some strengths. And those strengths will be in something about the decisions I will make, about the people I'll hang out with, for example, who could maybe understand what I am doing and give me help and support.

I wasn't Pelé. That nickname, thrown around with affection or teasing, wasn't something I questioned much in my younger years. It became part of the background noise of my identity, a label that neither weighed heavily nor propelled me forward. But as time passed, I began to realize that not being Pelé wasn't just about what I *wasn't*. It was about discovering who I *was*.

Adversity is a strange thing. Sometimes it announces itself loudly, like a storm rolling in with thunderous urgency. Other times, it's quiet, almost invisible, creeping into your life until one day you look around and realize you've been carrying its weight for years. For me, the adversity of defining my self-worth fell into the latter category. It wasn't down to one moment or event; it was a gradual realization that the world wasn't going to hand me a sense of identity. I had to create it for myself.

During that journey, I turned to heroes – not the kind that wore capes, but the ones that lived in books, movies and my imagination. Bruce Wayne taught me the value of preparation, the discipline to become stronger in every way. Sherlock Holmes showed me the power of curiosity and relentless observation. Agent 007 – James Bond – was my guide to confidence; always suave, but focused. And Albert Einstein, with his boundless creativity and courage to question the status quo, reminded me that the mind is our most powerful tool.

These weren't just idols; they were pieces of a vision I was building for myself. I began to see the man I wanted to become through their lenses. It wasn't about pretending to be them but using their strengths to shape my own narrative. That vision became my first step toward building self-worth.

Creating that vision wasn't easy. It required tough decisions. Deciding who added value to my life and who didn't. There were people who drained my energy, who kept me tethered to an old version of myself that no longer fit. Letting go of them wasn't about resentment, it was a matter of survival. To build something new, I had to make space for it.

And that's when I realized something profound: self-worth isn't something that appears out of thin air. It's built, piece by piece, with every choice we make about who we want to be and how we want to live. It's the foundation that supports us during life's greatest challenges and transitions.

Looking back, I can see that *not being Pelé* wasn't just a rejection of someone else's image of me – it was a declaration of who I was becoming. That journey of defining myself, of building my vision and protecting my self-worth, became a safety pillar that I lean on to this day.

Every leader, every person navigating change, must take this step. Before you can inspire others, before you can create a strategy or execute a plan, you must see yourself clearly. You must build a vision so strong and compelling that it pulls you forward, even when the road gets rough.

For me, that vision wasn't a single image. It was a mosaic of strengths drawn from everywhere – characters, mentors, experiences. It was about asking, "What if?" What if I prepared like Bruce Wayne? What if I questioned like Sherlock? What if I carried myself like 007 or imagined like Einstein? With every answer, I got closer to becoming the person I wanted to be.

This is what I've learned: adversity is a constant. It comes in waves, sometimes obvious, sometimes silent. But the power to overcome it lies within us, in the vision we create for our lives and the self-worth we build to support it.

You don't have to be Pelé. You just have to be you. And when you know who that is, when you create a vision so compelling it feels like destiny, no adversity can stand in your way.

CHAPTER 6

HOLMES, BOND, BATMAN ... AND EINSTEIN

I'd like to spend a bit more time talking about my childhood heroes – Sherlock Holmes, James Bond, Batman/Bruce Wayne and Albert Einstein – because they throw a lot of light on this central idea: the power of Logic, Emotion and Tactics (L.E.T.).

SHERLOCK HOLMES: THE POWER OF LOGIC AND OBSERVATION

When I first discovered Sherlock Holmes, I was captivated by his ability to uncover the truth in what seemed like impossible situations. His method was clear: **look at what is right in front of you, analyze the details and connect the dots.** That lesson has stayed with me throughout my life. Holmes taught me that the answers are often in plain sight if you know how to see them.

In my career, I've taken that lesson to heart. Whether I'm working with clients or managing complex negotiations, I try to emulate Holmes' relentless pursuit of clarity. His emphasis on **logic and observation** became the foundation of the L.E.T. model. Logic is where everything begins, whether solving a murder mystery or designing a business strategy.

But Holmes is more than just logic. What fascinates me is his subtle understanding of human emotion. While he seems cold and detached at times, he always considers the **emotional motivations** of the people he encounters. He knows that logic alone doesn't solve every problem; you have to understand the heart behind the actions. That's a crucial lesson for leadership: people are not equations to solve, they are dynamic, emotional beings.

Holmes also taught me the importance of **tactics**. When you're facing a challenge, it's not enough to have a strategy; you need the ability to adapt and execute with precision. Holmes' ability to read a situation and act decisively – whether it's a chess match with

Professor Moriarty or a high-stakes rescue – has shaped the way I approach challenges in business.

JAMES BOND: RESOURCEFULNESS AND ACTION

James Bond entered my life as the ultimate symbol of resourcefulness. No matter the situation, no matter how dire, Bond always found a way out. Whether it was using one of Q's gadgets or by sheer wit, Bond reminded me that there is always a solution if you're creative enough to see it.

In my life, I've often found myself in situations where the odds were stacked against me. Bond's influence is why I believe in my ability to think on my feet, to adapt in real-time, and to remain calm under pressure. He represents the **tactical execution** side of the L.E.T. framework – taking the logical strategy and putting it into action.

Bond is also a master of **building relationships** and leveraging them at the right time. His charm and confidence allow him to connect with people, even in the most hostile environments. That's something I've carried into my own leadership journey. In every negotiation or coaching session, I think of how Bond would approach the situation – calm, confident and always prepared.

Most importantly, 007 taught me to never give up. Even when the world seems to be collapsing around him, he stays focused on the mission. That sort of resilience has been crucial for me as a leader, especially during difficult times.

BRUCE WAYNE: THE BURDEN OF PURPOSE

As noted, Bruce Wayne has always been the character I relate to the most. His story is one of loss, pain and, ultimately, purpose. He didn't let the death of his parents define him; he turned his grief into a mission to bring justice to the world.

I've carried my own share of loss, and, like Bruce, I've felt the weight of that loss pushing me toward something bigger. He taught me that even when life seems overwhelming, you can channel that pain into something meaningful. In the L.E.T. framework, Bruce represents emotion – the deep, sometimes unspoken motivations that drive us to act.

What I admire most about Bruce Wayne is that he isn't a superhero because of his gadgets or his wealth; he's a superhero because of his determination and his unwavering sense of justice. He reminds me that leadership isn't about being perfect or invincible, it's about being willing to carry the burden of responsibility, even when it feels heavy.

Bruce also showed me the importance of duality. He wasn't just Batman, he was Bruce Wayne, the man behind the mask. In my own life, I've had to balance multiple roles – leader, father, partner – and Bruce taught me that it's OK to have different sides to who you are.

ALBERT EINSTEIN: THE BALANCE OF LOGIC AND EMOTION

Einstein's genius has always inspired me, not just because of his scientific breakthroughs but because of his **humanity**. He wasn't afraid to think differently, to challenge the norms, and to embrace his unique way of seeing the world. That willingness to be unconventional has shaped how I approach problems in both life and business.

What I find most fascinating about Einstein is his constant dance between **logic and emotion**. He wasn't just a brilliant scientist, he was also a deeply emotional person who saw beauty in the universe and believed in the power of imagination. That's a lesson I've woven into the L.E.T. framework. Leadership isn't just about numbers and plans, it's about vision, creativity and the ability to inspire others.

Einstein also faced rejection and criticism throughout his life. Despite his genius, there were times when people didn't understand or value his ideas. That taught me the importance of resilience and self-belief. Even when others doubt you, you have to stay true to your vision and keep moving forward.

HOW THESE FIGURES SHAPED ME AND THE L.E.T. MODEL

Each of these characters represents a key element of the L.E.T. framework:

- **Sherlock Holmes** embodies the **logic** needed to see the truth and create a clear strategy.
- **James Bond** exemplifies the **tactical execution** and adaptability required to turn plans into action.
- **Bruce Wayne** reminds me of the power of **emotion** – how our pain, purpose and humanity drive us to make a difference.
- **Albert Einstein** represents the balance of logic and emotion, showing that true leadership requires both intellect and imagination.

These figures have shaped not only who I am but also how I lead. They remind me that leadership is not one-dimensional. It's a blend of sharp thinking, emotional depth and decisive action.

There's something profoundly human about these inspirational figures who've shaped me. They are icons of brilliance, resourcefulness and purpose, but beneath the surface they carry a deep, often unspoken sadness. Their lives are dedicated to something greater than themselves, often at the cost of their own personal happiness. That thread of underlying loneliness – of being tethered to a mission larger than life – is something I've come to understand intimately.

Holmes, for all his genius, is isolated by it. He sees the world with such clarity that others often seem distant, unable to meet him on the same plane of thought. Wayne, haunted by the loss of his parents, channels his pain into justice but sacrifices the warmth of connection for the weight of his purpose. Bond, charming and confident as he is, operates in a world where relationships are fleeting, where the next mission always comes before the chance at a deeper connection.

There's a sweetness hidden within the loneliness of these iconic characters, a part of them that longs for connection, for love, for something beyond their purpose. Their stories remind us that even the most solitary souls have a place for love; a vulnerability that makes them deeply human. This part of them resonates with me just as much as their brilliance, their resourcefulness and their dedication to something greater than themselves.

Bruce Wayne, for all his darkness and his commitment to justice, loved Selina Kyle – Catwoman. In some stories, he's willing to give up everything for her. For a moment, his purpose, his pain and even his vow of vengeance take a back seat to the possibility of love. That willingness to embrace vulnerability, to risk his mission for connection, is something I deeply admire. It's a reminder that no matter how driven we are, love can soften us, heal us, and, at times, redefine our path.

Sherlock Holmes, often perceived as the coldest and most detached of them all, had his own soft spot: Irene Adler. "The Woman," as he called her, was the only person who could outwit him – and perhaps the only one who ever truly touched his heart. She represented an ideal for Holmes, not just intellectually but emotionally, someone who understood him in ways few could. That part of him – the quiet, unspoken yearning – reflects the human need to connect, even for someone as logical and guarded as Holmes.

And then there's James Bond. Beneath his suave, confident exterior, Bond loved Vesper Lynd with a depth that few people truly see. Her betrayal and death left a scar on him, one that shaped future relationships and his ability to trust. Yet, it's that love, however painful, that makes him more than just an agent on a mission. It's what reminds us that even the most fearless individuals carry their own heartbreaks, their own stories of love and loss.

These stories – the love of Selina, Irene and Vesper – bring a tenderness to these characters that I find profoundly moving. They remind me that even in a life filled with purpose and drive, love has the power to break through our walls, to touch the parts of us we think are untouchable. They remind me that, no matter how focused I am on my work, my journey or my mission, love is what gives life its meaning.

And then there's Albert Einstein, a man of unmatched intellect who seemed to love fiercely, both in his work and in his personal life. His passion for discovery, for questioning the universe, was mirrored in his tumultuous love life – split between two wives and multiple affairs, marked by intense, imperfect relationships. It's a reminder that even the most brilliant minds wrestle with the complexities of the heart.

I see myself in all of them. I love my work, my journey and the purpose that fuels me. My passion for what I do drives me to push boundaries, to create something meaningful, to pave the way for others, especially my children. But there's an undeniable tradeoff. Like my heroes, I've felt the pull of a mission that can sometimes eclipse the personal.

I adore my children. Everything I do, every step I take, is with them in mind. I want to set a course for them that's not just smooth but inspiring – a path they can walk with confidence and pride. And yet, as much as I love them, I often ask myself if I've found the right balance between my purpose and my presence in their lives. That question lingers, just as it must have for Einstein, whose genius often came at the cost of time and connection.

Love, for me, is both a curse and a blessing. I love to love, whether it's my work, the people in my life or the vision I'm trying to bring to reality. But I'm scared of loving, too. Scared of giving so much that I lose myself, or of holding back for fear of losing what I give. It's a tension I've carried, much like the fictional heroes I admire. Their loneliness resonates because I've felt it too. Loving deeply is a vulnerability, and yet it's also where I find my greatest strength.

These characters have taught me that loneliness is not the enemy. It's often the byproduct of purpose, of striving to make a difference, to live beyond yourself. But they've also taught me that, even in loneliness, there is connection. Holmes had Watson. Bond, as fleeting as his relationships were, still touched lives. Bruce, despite his dark path, inspired hope in others. And Einstein, for all his struggles, left a legacy not just of knowledge but of curiosity and wonder.

Their stories remind me to embrace the contradictions in my own life. To love fiercely, even when it's scary. To carry my purpose with pride, even when it feels heavy. To stay humble, knowing that the journey isn't just about me – it's about the lives I touch, the roads I help pave, and the love I give along the way.

In the L.E.T. framework, these lessons come together. **Logic** gives me the clarity to see the path ahead. **Emotion** fuels my connection to others and my drive to inspire. And **Tactics** remind me to act decisively, even when the road is uncertain. Together, they form a blueprint – not for perfection, but for purpose.

I am not Holmes, Bond, Wayne or Einstein. Still, I carry pieces of them in me, and they've shaped who I am today. They have shown me that greatness doesn't come without struggle, that love is worth the fear it brings, and that a life dedicated to something greater than yourself is a life worth living. Through them, I've learned that the most important journey isn't about solving mysteries, saving the world or unravelling the secrets of the universe – it's about finding the courage to love, to lead and to leave the world just a little better than you found it.

CHAPTER 7

ROCK BOTTOM

Back in Querétaro, I took a sabbatical year. I had decided I wanted to go to veterinary school and train to be a vet. I wanted to work on ranches with large animals – horses and cattle rather than with small animals such as people's cats and dogs and rabbits. I started working with a cousin who was a vet for the ranches, and I also ran a small hotel that was owned by another cousin, doing literally everything: I was the manager, the receptionist and the cleaner, all rolled into one.

After about six months, I started vet school. I did that for about six months, and it taught me two things. The first was that being a vet would be a very difficult career if you didn't have a good existing relationship with a ranch. It was a hard industry to break into and I didn't want to have to rely on calling in favors from family and friends, who could introduce me to ranch owners. The second thing I learned was that I was too soft-hearted to be a vet.

I once went out on a call to a ranch with my cousin, the vet, to help with a cow that was having complications giving birth to a calf. We arrived at the ranch at maybe 4:00 in the morning and examined the cow, and the rancher said, "What have we got here? How much is it going to cost for this procedure?" The problem was that the calf was in an abnormal position, and my cousin told him the cost to try to deliver it successfully. The rancher said it wasn't worth the expense. He had perhaps 800 cows, and the cost of saving this one animal and its calf was not worth it. He would prefer to put the cow down. He was making a business decision. Ranching is a tough business and there's not much room for sentimentality.

But I just lost it. I just couldn't allow that to happen. I had to try to save the cow and its calf. My cousin was telling me that this was just a fact of life on the ranch, but I was saying, "There's a ranch I know and I'm sure they will take this cow, and we can deliver the calf..." The rancher was fine with that. He said, "I don't care what you guys do as long as I don't get charged." We ended up taking the cow to another ranch, where we managed to deliver the calf and, I am absolutely certain, mother and child lived happily ever after.

But my cousin said, "Mau, we can't do this every time a rancher wants to put an animal down rather than pay for treatment. It's not viable." I agreed. "You're right," I told him. "But this is not for me. If they're gonna ask me to do that kind of thing, I'm not gonna be able to do it." And that was the end of my veterinary career.

I switched from vet studies to tourism administration. Tourism is big in Mexico, and I had some small experience of the hotel business. But to be honest, my main motivation was that I could see myself running a nice hotel where lots of pretty ladies would turn up for their vacation and there I would be, waiting to greet them. As visions of the future go, it was a good vision. It gave me the motivation to persevere in my studies. But I can see now that it lacked depth.

After about a year and a half of tourism studies, I started to get a more mature outlook. I thought, "Well, hotels are businesses. If I study business, I can maybe decide to manage a hotel, but I will have other options open to me than just tourism." So I switched to a degree in business administration. It was one of the best decisions of my life. I began to realize I had found my vocation in life.

I worked during the whole time I was studying so I could pay my way. I worked as fleet manager for a gas company that delivered fuel to people's houses. The tanker trucks would roll up and fill their tanks, and my job was to make sure the fleet was well-maintained and staffed and running smoothly.

When I finished my degree in business administration, I got a job with a small veterinary pharmaceutical company run by some of my cousins. They were importing medicines from the US. The job appealed to me because I had some knowledge of pharmaceuticals from my veterinary studies. It involved doing all the registration and licensing needed to be able to introduce the medicines to the Mexican market, which was a complex and rigorous process that involved dealing with government agencies. Once that was all sorted and running smoothly, I was given responsibility for marketing the products and talking to potential distributors.

I enjoyed the job, but the starting salary had not been very good. Once we had distribution organized and the import business was beginning to run properly and make money, I asked for a raise. It was a modest raise, and it was entirely justified, but they refused. Their attitude was: "You just graduated, and you are Mauricio. You're family! Come on, we've given you this opportunity, and this salary is all you need!"

I felt I was still being seen as the young person I had always been. "You know: 'Pelé!' Espinosa's boy!" I always felt the subtext was, "He's never going to amount to much, but he's a good kid and we've taken him on," even though I had my degree, and I knew I had a lot more to offer. I felt I was always the nephew or the cousin ... the *someone* of *somebody*. I felt I was being dragged back into the situation I had wanted to avoid when I was thinking of becoming a vet – of always needing to know someone who could call in a favor to get me work on a good ranch. I never felt known as just me, myself. By my name, Mauricio. By who I was, and what I could contribute through my knowledge and my skills.

I decided to leave the family business and got a job at a bank. I started out as a teller. I took all the training courses that the bank made available and found some great mentors there. My boss's boss in particular really seemed to believe in me. I quickly got promoted and became general manager of one of the bank's branches when I was 27 years old – the youngest manager in the area. I loved the world of business and finance, and I was hungry to learn as much as I could, so I signed up for a course in economics at the Autonomous University of Querétaro.

Now that I was the general manager of a bank branch, my family and friends began to take an interest in me again. They started to come by and open accounts at my branch. I was proud of that; I felt I was showing everyone what I was capable of. But by being trusting and open, as a naïve 27-year-old, and being led (at the time) more by emotions than by logic, I fell into a web of lies and manipulation that ended up with me leaving the bank with my reputation ruined – or that's how it felt to me at the time.

There were two cousins in particular who I really looked up to. I saw them as people to admire; as role models. But they took advantage of me and got me into big trouble. When you love and admire someone, when you open yourself up to someone like that, you don't think logically. You don't notice that the emotional return for you is negative; that everything is flowing one way.

One morning, I was working at my branch of the bank when I got a phone call from the legal department. "Hey, Mau, don't go anywhere," they said. "We're going to come and do an audit at your branch." Audits happen. They made it sound like a very routine operation. "Sure," I said. "Of course. I'll be waiting for you."

A short while later, a kind of SWAT team burst into the bank, carrying rifles. The armed guys hung around, looking menacing, while the auditors fired questions at me. It was about checks drawn on my cousins' accounts. These checks had needed what was known as 'double authorization.' I had requested the authorization, and it had always been given, so I had assumed everything was fine – which was what my cousins had told me: "These checks might need double authorization, but that's all normal. If you just make the application, it will be fine." I told this to the auditors. I told them I had called various departments to see if I could pay the checks and they said yes, so I assumed everything was OK.

It wasn't OK. The guys with guns took me to jail, and I was held there for four or five hours before my dad arrived with an attorney. The attorney could show that I was not guilty of anything, that I hadn't done anything illegal. What I had done was trust my cousins and been persuaded by them to do something that, in effect, fell between the bank's processes. After everything settled down,

I talked to other managers who told me that if anything needed double authorization, they wouldn't touch it, just to cover themselves. But I didn't know that at the time.

There was a piece in the local newspaper about my arrest, complete with my photograph. A week later, the bank released a statement saying that it had all been a misunderstanding and that nothing criminal had taken place. However, the statement was small, with no picture, buried on an inside page, and all people remembered was that I had been hauled away and spent time in the cells. And I still lost my job, because, although it may have been a misunderstanding, the bank was not happy.

The following week, another bad thing happened to me.

I had a girlfriend in Querétaro. I was crazy about her. I went back to visit her one time, planning to propose that we get engaged to be married. I took some flowers and I had this idea that I would leave the flowers in her car, because she had given me a key to her car, and she would get a nice surprise when she got in her car to come and meet me.

But when I arrived at her car, it was rocking slightly on its suspension and the windows were all misted up inside. I don't think I need to describe the situation any further, other than to say that my girlfriend was in the back seat, and she was not alone. She saw me standing outside the car, staring at the misted windows, and came rushing out of the car to meet me, adjusting her clothes, but there was nothing to be said. I left and went home.

In the course of just over a week, I had been accused of criminality, been arrested by guys carrying rifles, spent a few hours in a jail cell, had my photo in the newspapers as a potential criminal and found my fiancé-to-be ... well, let's just say that I had broken up with my fiancé-to-be.

That weekend, a friend called to tell me he was having a party at his ranch, and asked if I wanted to come over and have some drinks. And I said of course I wanted to come over and have some drinks at the ranch.

So I was at the ranch and I was getting hammered when I got a phone call from some other friends, because all of them knew I was at the ranch. And these other friends said, "Hey, Mau, we're in downtown Querétaro and there's some girls over here and you need to come join us." And I'm like, "I'll be there in ten minutes."

The normal ride from the ranch to downtown is around 40 minutes and, obviously, I was not going to make it in ten minutes, but the roads are deserted at that time of night, and you think you can get there in ten minutes because you're drunk, you're young and you're stupid. I got in my car and started to drive to Querétaro.

In Mexico back then, when they were doing some repairs to the roads, they sometimes forgot to put up signs warning motorists about the road work ahead. Or maybe there's a small sign that says, "Roadworks Ahead," but it doesn't tell you what work is being done and it's a small sign and you're drunk.

Turns out they were doing some repairs to a bridge, and the bridge wasn't there anymore. They had removed the bridge in order to fix it.

When I drove onto the bridge that wasn't there anymore, the car went airborne. It flew over the ravine and crashed into a tree on the far side, and I was thrown out of the back window of the car.

The only reason I'm alive today is that I was not wearing a seat belt – the once-in-a-thousand times that not being buckled in might save your life. After I was thrown clear, the car hit the ground roof-first and somersaulted several times. I remember opening my eyes and realizing I was lying in a field. I remembered being in the car, and now I was lying in a field, and I could see the car, upside down, maybe five or six meters away from me in the field and I didn't know where I was or what had happened.

I had another stroke of luck. A truck driver was on the same road (so people do drive those roads at night, after all) but he was sober, and he had not driven off the bridge that wasn't there, but he had seen me fly off it. He called an ambulance, and they came and found me. As they were taking me to hospital, they found my ID in my wallet and called my parents. When the medics first got to me in the field, they thought I was dead. While I was in the ambulance, they kept poking me in the arm to keep me awake because they didn't want me to pass out again. I remember being poked, and how cross that made me.

My dad was at the hospital when the ambulance arrived. He could hear me shouting inside the ambulance and he told me later that the shouting let him know I was still alive. He said to himself, "OK, he's alive. He's drunk as hell, but he's alive." But I was shouting about how my back hurt, and he was worried about whether I had broken my back. Then they opened the back doors of the ambulance, and the paramedic came flying out the door because I had kicked him because I was angry that he kept poking me. My dad thought, "Well, his legs are still working. That's a good sign."

The next day, my dad went with someone from the insurance company to look at the car. The insurance guy told dad that he had all the paperwork to claim for the car being totalled, as well as the forms for him to be able to claim life insurance on me, and he would need the death certificate and so on. And my dad told him that I was not dead, and the insurance guy was very solicitous, and he said that he understood in situations like this it was very difficult to come to terms with things and he was so sorry – because he was so certain that no one could walk away from a crash like that. My dad had to bring him to the hospital to see me before he'd believe that I was actually alive.

I went home from hospital, and I was physically OK apart from some cuts and bruises but, mentally, I was in a bad way. I was questioning the point of my existence. I had been through a terrible accident and I had survived when I should have been dead, but I wasn't sure that was a good thing and whether there was any point in my being alive.

I had lost my job. My picture had been in the paper because I had been in jail, and everybody remembered the picture but no one remembered the statement that came later saying it had all been a misunderstanding. I'd lost the girl I thought was the love of my life. I wasn't going to have a job. Nobody believed in me except my parents. I was thinking that I would be nobody in this life. People had been right – I wasn't going to amount to anything. Professionally and personally, I was broken. The self-esteem I had gained from my time in America was gone. A night of drinking and driving had led to a terrible accident that almost cost me my life. I was at my parents' house recovering, but I didn't want to see anyone. I didn't want to talk. I was done. Everyone was right, I was just Pelé after all, and I should just embrace it.

I was lying on a couch in my parents' house watching TV. There was a football game on, but I couldn't get involved in it. Nothing seemed to matter. Everything seemed gray and pointless. My mother was in the lounge next door, watching something else on another TV.

I suppose what happened next was a dream, because nobody else remembers it or saw anything. But a nun came into my room – the kind of nun you get teaching kids at Catholic schools. Just an ordinary nun. Tiny but fierce. Takes no nonsense and terrifies all the kids into doing what they're supposed to be doing. She grabbed me by the shirt. I can feel her tugging at my shirt to this day and can see her in my mind, clear as crystal. She was shouting right in my face and using the kind of language that I'm afraid I used to use – which was very surprising to me, because she was a nun.

"Stop fucking complaining, you motherfucker!" she shouted, tightening her grip. "Stop your bullshit and start living your life! You have it in you to be whatever you want, so stop your fucking crap and start living!"

The nun let go my shirt and left. I lay there on the couch, stunned. I couldn't believe it. What was happening? When I think back on that amazing afternoon, I have to decide it wasn't real. It never happened. No one else saw her come into the house or leave. But whatever it was – a dream or a vision – it was my wakeup call.

It worked.

The next day, I told my parents I had to go somewhere else and get things figured out. I went to stay at the house of an uncle who lived in a different city and then decided to go back to Kansas. To the place where I had gained my self-esteem. The place called Protection that had offered me protection when I was younger.

After a couple of weeks there, one of my friends told me he was going to Kansas City because he was thinking of studying there. He was going to stay with a cousin who lived there. I wasn't doing anything apart from hanging out in Protection, so I asked if I could join him and see something of Kansas City, and he said, "Sure. Let me check with my cousin and his wife if that's OK by them, but sure." He made the call and said that was fine by them and his cousin had asked what my background was, and he had told them about my degree in business administration and my experience at the bank (the good bits, not the one bad bit!) and his cousin had asked if I could send him my resume.

My friend and I were both 26 or 27 years old at the time, and I assumed his cousin was the same age, and I wondered why he would want to see my resume, but I didn't think much about it, and I sent a copy on ahead of our arrival, figuring it's always good to get your resume out there.

It turned out that my friend's cousin was older than us and was CEO of a company in Kansas City called NCM Associates that specialized in peer-to-peer networking in the auto industry. By chance, the company had just been asked by Ford Motor Company to start the first 20 Group in Mexico (I mentioned earlier how NCM had pioneered the idea of creating groups of 20 auto dealers who would come together to exchange ideas on best practice). The CEO wondered if I might be useful as a financial analyst for the new international division.

We stayed at my friend's cousin's house for a couple of nights, and dinner on the first night turned into a kind of interview for me between him and his wife. His wife knew a lot about me because of their links with Protection, which is a tiny place where everyone knows everything about everyone else, and she seemed to like me, as did her husband. He asked me if I could have another interview the next day with his Director of International Operations, a guy named Tony Noland. I took the interview, and Tony obviously liked me enough to offer me the job. Tony went on to become my biggest mentor, and the person who taught me everything about the auto industry.

Tony sent me back to Mexico and asked me to do a market study of the auto industry there while they applied for my green card, and six months later I was back in the US with a green card and a job and a plan.

It meant a lot that the company believed in me as a person, without really knowing anything about me. Everything they knew came from my resume, job application form and the conversations with the CEO and his wife and my interview with Tony. They liked my personality, and they liked what I said, and they hired me. It was the first time in my life when I felt I had been accepted for the person I was, and not as the person everyone thought they knew all about. It felt like my first real job. I had an enormous desire to succeed with this company – and to succeed in a different country, in a different language, with a different culture. I wasn't simply determined; I had created a clear vision and an internal narrative. I started work in my new company determined with the clear idea that I was either going to be successful, or I was going to go back to Mexico with my tail between my legs. If I didn't succeed with this company, I would leave Kansas City and head back to Mexico as a failure. And I told myself that was never going to happen.

There's something raw and humbling about hitting rock bottom. It's a place where everything feels stripped away – your confidence, your plans, your sense of direction. Falling that far isn't just a stumble; it's a freefall that leaves you gasping for air, unsure if you'll ever rise again. And yet, falling is also universal. We all have our version of it.

Reading Viktor E. Frankl's book *Man's Search for Meaning* reminded me of this universality. Frankl was an Austrian psychologist and philosopher, and a survivor of the holocaust and the Nazi death camps. Frankl's unimaginable suffering and resilience in the face of incomprehensible horrors put my struggles into perspective. My rock bottom was nothing compared to the depths of despair he endured, yet the lessons remain relevant. Because, while most of us will never face the profound agony of a concentration camp, we all experience moments when life seems to strip us of everything we hold dear.

For me, the most profound realization about falling was this: it's not the end. It's a chapter, not the whole story. And, just as Frankl discovered meaning even in his suffering, I began to see that rock bottom has its own lessons, about resilience, perspective and the surprising strength of the human spirit.

One of those lessons is about people. In my lowest moments, I began to notice something remarkable: the people around me – family, friends, mentors, even strangers – became anchors, lifelines I could grab onto when the current felt too strong. Some of them knew exactly how to help, offering guidance and support. Others helped in quieter ways, simply by being there, reminding me I wasn't alone.

Psychologists call this social support, and it's one of the most critical factors in navigating adversity. When we fall, our instinct might be to isolate ourselves, to retreat into our own pain. But it's precisely in those moments that reaching out becomes essential. Whether it's a friend who listens without judgement, a mentor who offers perspective, or even a professional therapist who provides tools for growth, the people around us play an irreplaceable role in our journey upward.

There's also something to be said about the roles we assign to these people, intentionally or not. In those moments, I wasn't always looking for someone to fix everything; I was looking for someone to walk alongside me. A conversation, a shared silence, even a gesture of understanding became a source of strength. It taught me that leadership isn't just about leading others, it's also about allowing others to lead us when we need it most.

Another lesson of rock bottom is about control, or the lack of it. Some falls come from our own mistakes; others blindside us with their randomness. Life, as much as we try to control it, often reminds us that it operates on its own terms. But here's the truth I've come to embrace: while we can't always control what happens to us, we can control how we respond.

This is where resilience comes into play. Psychologists define resilience as the ability to bounce back from adversity, to adapt and thrive despite challenges. It's not about avoiding the fall but learning how to rise from it. And rising doesn't mean pretending the fall didn't happen. It means acknowledging it, learning from it and choosing to move forward.

Frankl wrote that "life is never made unbearable by circumstances, but only by lack of meaning and purpose." When I hit rock bottom, I didn't need grand answers or instant solutions. I needed a reason to take the next step, however small it seemed. And as I began to climb, I realized that meaning isn't something you find. It's something you create.

For me, creating meaning meant leaning into my network, allowing myself to be vulnerable and finding small victories to celebrate. It meant seeing the fall not as a failure but as a chance to rebuild with greater clarity and strength. And, most importantly, it meant recognizing that rock bottom isn't a permanent address. It's a temporary stop on the way to something better.

We all fall. We all face moments when life feels too heavy a burden to carry. But if there's one thing I've learned, it's that falling doesn't define us. Rising does. And we don't rise alone. We rise with the people who love us, the lessons we learn, and the belief that even at rock bottom, there's a way forward.

If you're in that place – if life has knocked you down and you're wondering how to move forward – look to the people around you. Allow them to guide you, to remind you of your worth and your potential. Take one step, and then another. Create your meaning. And know that the fall is never the end. It's just part of the journey.

CHAPTER 8

NEW BEGINNINGS

I had been hired at NCM Associates as a financial analyst and assistant to the director of the International Division, which consisted of three people: Tony Nolan, my boss, and one executive coach, with me supplying financial analysis and anything else that might help them get more business and keep existing clients happy. And that was fine by me. I was excited about the opportunity, excited about the job, about what they were doing. I was helping them develop the non-US market, in Mexico and Europe.

I had visualized to myself that I had just two years to become an executive coach. I've always been a fan of visualization: vision over goals. Without a vision, goals have no substance, and if I could not realize my vision I would have to go back to Mexico, which, for me, was not even remotely an option. I had told myself that if I didn't get made up to executive coach, I would go back to Mexico exactly 48 hours before the second anniversary of the day I started the job. That date was seared in my brain. But I didn't just wait, and hope to get promoted. I had data on all of our clients – that was my job – and I remember thinking, what do the coaches do? They ask me for an analysis, I take them through the data, and explain everything as best I can, and give them some possible options based on my reading of the data. Then they call the clients. Their years of expertise and the financial data I had supplied created a great process for success.

Then I thought, well, I don't have the experience, but I do have the knowledge. And, if you think about it, the clients have the experience, because nobody knows their own business better than they do. What they needed was the new perspective on their business that more data could give them, and if I could provide that, and show them what the data was telling me about where there was scope for their business to improve, they could use their experience to make the final decision.

That gave me the courage to try approaching clients myself. I started to make phone calls and try to get put through to the head of the company. I don't remember how many companies I called or how many people I emailed; I knew I needed just one opportunity. But time was running out. It got to the point where there were only weeks left before my self-imposed deadline expired, and I would have to admit defeat and return to Mexico.

Whenever I could get through to a business owner directly, I would tell them what I saw in their numbers, and that I had some ideas about what they could do to make more money. And one day, literally two weeks before my deadline was about to expire, one of those guys said, “Hold on, if you’re telling me I could be making more money, I’d like to hear what you have to say. Can you come here to meet me?” I went to Tony and asked if I could make the journey, and he said, “Of course you can. If the client is willing to pay for your travel, you’re free to go. Are you ready?”

Boy, was I ready. And off I went, with just my expenses covered. The company didn’t charge for my time, because I wasn’t yet a consultant, I was just a financial analyst. Was I scared? I was terrified. I was 29 years old, and I was going into the office of a well-known car dealer in Mexico to tell him what I had found in the data, what I thought he could do better and how that could change his operation. I knew I could do the job, and, emotionally, I was set. But I was still scared.

I went and I showed the company my figures. But figures without context are just data, so I had to convert the data into decision-making points. I had to create business intelligence, a concept that was still developing at the time. Back then, it was all about data. Then came information, followed by intelligence, and, finally, decisions made from data. That’s what I was providing, along with what I thought they could do to improve things. We compared ideas, and I asked about their projections and the basis for them, and we discussed that. And in the end, they adopted my recommendations.

When I showed the results to my company on Tuesday, November 3, 1998, they promoted me to executive coach, and they were able to start charging a fee for what I did.

I had achieved my goal. I had made decisions tactically and logically. For me to get the job I wanted, I had to show I could earn it. That was a tactical decision. I had the knowledge, so I knew the logic of the situation. I knew I could present the data and show what could be achieved, in a clear, logical way. And I had the emotional drive to see the whole thing through and reach my goal.

Today, I tell many young executives this part of my story to illustrate the power of vision and narrative to help us achieve goals. When you define where you want to go in life, set a reasonable timeframe and analyze exactly what you want – the job, situation or lifestyle you desire, whatever it might be – and tell yourself a compelling narrative about exactly how you're going to make that happen ... If you do all that, with a powerful vison and narrative, then you don't just 'try your best,' you do everything that needs to be done to achieve the vision. You *will* make it happen. In my own case, I gave myself a narrative about how I would have to return to Mexico as a failure if I had not achieved promotion within two years of starting with the company. That was not just a vague hope, it was a promise – a *threat* – to my future self. I was never going to allow that to happen. It gave me all the motivation I needed.

From my earliest days at NCM, I had studied the executive consultants in the main, US division there. I would go into their offices and ask questions. They used to call me 'the why? guy,' because every time they gave me an answer, I would ask, *"Why?"* It was a simple question that challenges the status quo. Tony would spend hours with me, explaining things and answering questions, and I spent weeks asking questions of all the consultants and others, who were always happy to help. What a great tool to use: questions. I was like a sponge, asking questions and learning, absorbing all the information I was given.

Tony also arranged for me to work in various car dealerships to build up my knowledge of the business. I would work at the consultancy from maybe 8:30 to 5:30, then do an evening shift at a dealership starting at 6:00. I would also work the showrooms on Saturdays, working and learning, selling some cars and making some money on the side. In time, I started to shadow the managers of these businesses and learn how they ran their operations. That helped me to understand the industry much better. As a consultant, knowing the numbers is your stock in trade. And then comes understanding your clients' business. But to this day I remember Tony saying to me, "You will never know more about the business than the client does. The client knows his own business better than anybody." I learned that my job was to know my numbers and understand the wider business context as best I could and then provide business owners with the right questions. If I could find the right questions, they would come back with the right answers, and I would have helped them move forward and break new ground.

The boss of that initial car dealership in Mexico, who trusted me and listened to what I had to say and accepted my recommendations, is still a client of mine, all these years later. I have helped him grow his business, and I have coached his kids, who are in their 40s now and extremely successful in their own right, as part of the consultancy team that my own company now supplies. Nearly 30 years later, he's still a client of mine.

Life in the US started going well for me. I was generating good business for the company, bringing in new clients and helping the clients improve their business so they were happy with our service and stayed with us.

I started building the whole American dream for myself. I got married. My wife had a four-year-old daughter by her first marriage, and I adopted her as my own child. Later, we had kids of our own. Then we got divorced, I went broke, and I had to start all over again.

Around that time, NCM was going through a lot of mergers and acquisitions (M&A), and I didn't want to miss out on that. I started to help the company with potential acquisitions while I was still working as a consultant for the international division. I used to run all the financial data on target companies. If there was serious interest in any of the target companies, then conversations would begin, and these would involve a lot of negotiation, which I enjoyed. I decided I wanted to learn more about negotiation, and that I wanted to learn from the best. I saw that Harvard Business School had a negotiation program, so I signed up for that. I was working full time, and I was married and we were thinking of starting a family, but I made a tactical decision. I wanted to go where I could learn from the best teachers and study alongside the brightest and most challenging fellow students. So, I went to Harvard Business School. It was expensive, but I saw it as an investment; a tactical decision. It paid off. I learned a huge amount about negotiation and about sales, and I later created a sales training program based on my new knowledge. We still use it at my company today.

I continued to work as a coach for the company's international division, and to help with their M&A activities. One of my colleagues, Chris, who was running the used car division, moved to another company in Sarasota, Florida. I was talking to him about his move, and he said, "I'd like you to come and work with us over here. It's going to be a great company." And my response was that I would love to, but I loved what I had created in the international division, and I didn't want to leave it. And he said, "Well, let's buy that division!" Because NCM was undertaking a major restructuring, making new acquisitions but also being open to the possibility of selling off some of their existing divisions. We created a plan to buy out their international division, which was accepted, and I was presented with the option to move to the new company as director of a new International Division, in Sarasota. My clients had all agreed to move over to the new company with me. I decided to take the opportunity, and my wife and I moved to Florida with our daughter, our dog Athos (a miniature schnauzer) and Tommy, our black cat.

Everything was working out nicely. I was happily married. Our first baby, a boy, was born. We were living in The Sunshine State. Everything went wonderfully for about three years. And then the dot.com bubble burst in 2000, the stock market crashed, and there was 9/11.

The shock of those events brought on many financial pressures and created the need for change. In 2001, with Chris and two other executives, we created another new company, and then, in 2003, I bought out my partners to create my own business, which is the company I have today: G20, Inc. Another tactical decision, again made with the full support of my clients. And with that, we moved back to Kansas City.

There was a very memorable event at that time. Not a happy event, but something that taught me a lot about myself. I was in Mexico City, about to give a motivational speech, when I got a call from my wife. We were expecting another baby, and she had miscarried. I was 1,400 miles from home and due on stage in 20 minutes. There was nothing I could do immediately. My wife and I talked for a while and she told me, "Go make the speech, because you have 250 people waiting to hear you. Then come home."

And I did. I went out there and gave one of the best speeches I've ever delivered, judging from the amount of applause from the people attending and from people in my own company who told me I'd really been at the top of my form. And when I told my colleagues about the phone call from my wife, they couldn't believe it.

I think that was the moment I understood what being resilient meant, and what it gives you. It becomes clear what you can control and what you cannot. Resilience gives you the fuel to help yourself do what you can to the best of your abilities, using what you know and what makes you feel proud of yourself.

Resilience is not an emotion, although some people think of it that way. It is a characteristic or trait that allows one to withstand or recover quickly from difficult conditions. Emotions are temporary states that can change frequently, such as happiness, sadness, anger or fear. Resilience, on the other hand, is a more stable quality that influences how a person responds to and manages their emotions in the face of adversity.

Managing my emotions that day and showing resilience was not the first time I had ever done it in my life, but it was the first time

I had done it consciously and with a purpose. Later, in many phases of my life, I have been able to stay resilient by drawing on that inner reserve. I'm constantly learning about my life. I do a lot of reflection. Over time I've learned to put everything into the silos of Logic, Emotion and Tactics. Back then, I was only beginning to understand the type of decisions I was making, the sort of data I had in order to make decisions, and my emotional state at any point.

New beginnings often feel like a clean slate – an opportunity to start fresh, full of optimism and possibility. But they can also feel overwhelming. Where do you begin? How do you ensure that this time will be different? What will stop you from falling into the same patterns that didn't serve you before?

As I reflected on the concept of new beginnings, I realized something crucial: they don't just happen. They're not simply handed to us like a gift we unwrap. They're built, deliberately and carefully, with strategy, structure and a system that works for you.

I've learned this the hard way. In the past, I'd dive headfirst into a new project or venture, fuelled by excitement but lacking a solid plan. And more often than not, that initial spark of enthusiasm would fizzle out, leaving me frustrated and stuck. What changed? It wasn't my ambition or my passion – it was my approach. I stopped relying on sheer willpower to get me through and started relying on a process.

Here's the thing about processes and systems: they're not exciting. They're not glamorous. But they're essential. They provide the structure and stability you need to turn your goals into reality. Think about it like building a house. You don't just grab a hammer and start nailing boards together. You need a blueprint, a foundation, and a clear understanding of what you're building. Without those, even the most beautiful design will collapse.

In this chapter of my journey, I learned to embrace the power of planning and strategy. I began asking myself questions that weren't always easy to answer. What do I really want? What steps will get me there? What obstacles might I face, and how will I overcome them? These questions forced me to think critically and act intentionally.

Psychologists and organizational experts often talk about the concept of *self-efficacy* – the belief in your ability to achieve a specific goal. It's not just about confidence; it's about competence. And competence grows when you combine belief in yourself with a clear, actionable plan. For me, that combination became a turning point.

With a renewed sense of self-worth and a deeper understanding of who I was, I began to see planning not as a chore but as an act of self-respect. It was a way of saying, "I believe in myself enough to take this seriously. I'm not just hoping for success, I'm preparing for it."

I started by breaking my goals into smaller, manageable steps. Instead of focusing on the end result, I focused on the next action I could take. This shift was liberating. Suddenly, the mountain I wanted to climb didn't seem so daunting. It was just a series of steps, each one building on the last.

I also realized the importance of creating a system that worked for me. Not one that worked for someone else or looked good on paper, but one that fit my unique strengths, habits and lifestyle. This meant being honest about my limitations and designing a process that accounted for them. It wasn't about perfection; it was about progress.

Research in habit formation, particularly by experts like James Clear, author of *Atomic Habits*, reinforces this idea. Clear explains that small, consistent actions compound over time to create significant results. The key is not to rely solely on motivation, which can be fleeting, but to create systems that make success inevitable.

One of the most valuable lessons I learned was the importance of flexibility. Even the best-laid plans will encounter obstacles. Life has a way of throwing curveballs, and rigidity can be a recipe for frustration. I had to learn to adapt my strategy without abandoning my vision. This required not just planning but *adaptive planning* – the ability to adjust and pivot while staying focused on the bigger picture.

As I reflect on this chapter of my life, I'm struck by how empowering it felt to take control of my journey. There's a profound sense of satisfaction that comes from knowing you're not just drifting through life, hoping for the best. You're steering the ship, charting your course, and navigating with purpose.

If you're standing at the threshold of a new beginning, here's what I'd share with you:

1. **Define Your Vision**
   Be clear about what you want and why it matters to you. Your vision is the foundation of your journey.

2. **Break It Down**
   Turn your vision into actionable steps. Focus on progress, not perfection.

3. **Build a System**
   Create a structure that works for you. Use tools, habits and routines that align with your strengths and needs.

4. **Stay Adaptable**
   Be prepared to adjust your plan as circumstances change. Flexibility is not a sign of weakness, it's a hallmark of resilience.

5. **Trust the Process**
   Believe in the system you've created and give yourself time to see the results.

New beginnings are not about wiping the slate clean and starting over from scratch. They're about building on what you've learned, leveraging your strengths, and creating a path that aligns with your values and aspirations. With the right mindset and a solid plan, you can turn any new beginning into a powerful chapter of growth and achievement.

The journey is yours to design. So, what will you build?

CHAPTER 9

EATING TUNA OUT THE TIN

In 2003 we were in Kansas City and I had started my own company and the company was doing well. Our first child, Dany, had been born in 2000. Our son, Joseph, was born in 2004 ... but our marriage was not going so well. In 2005 our third child, Emma, was born, but things with our marriage were not getting better. We decided finally to separate, but it was not an amicable separation. My wife filed for divorce in September 2008. On September 15, Lehman Bothers filed for bankruptcy, following risky investment in mortgages and poor management. On September 29, the Dow Jones Industrial Average fell almost 778 points, the largest drop in history at that time. The 2008 financial crash was gathering pace, the Great Recession was about to begin, and I was getting divorced

The immediate effects of the crash brought my income down by 60%. No one knew how badly businesses would be affected in the longer term. The credit crunch kicked in almost immediately. Everyone was stunned. I had no contingency plan in place for my business, and with my personal life on the line, I hadn't been following what was happening in the world. The financial meltdown took me by surprise. (My fault, I should have seen it coming, and I didn't do my job). In one week, I lost 60% of my revenue and it was like a waterfall of emotions that blinded all logical thinking.

Then, one day, I checked the company bank account, and it was empty. My business partner had taken all the cash out. He knew I had personal difficulties. I guess he didn't know if the business would pull through, so he must have decided, "The future doesn't look so good. I'll take this money as my compensation for being a partner in this company." He took all the money and disappeared.

I had no choice but to lay off my colleagues, the business's executive coaches. The only person I was able to keep on the books was my assistant, who has been with me through thick and thin – and this was a very thin period. I had to sell the family house on a short sale and find a rental house for my wife and kids and an apartment for myself. Not only did I sell the house, I had to sell nearly all my furniture. When I moved into my own rented apartment,

I had four pieces of furniture: a bed, a table and two chairs. I also had a fridge and a cooker. That was about it.

I was facing a lot of legal bills because of the divorce. My expenses had increased 100%, because now I had two households to finance, but my income had crashed. My business partner had emptied the business bank account. I began to fall behind on my taxes and general living expenses. I didn't file for Chapter 11 bankruptcy protection. It would have made financial sense, but I didn't want to go that route.

There was something else.

Because of the legal action surrounding the divorce, I was not allowed to leave the US. My soon-to-be ex-wife was making a claim on my estate and my earnings, and her lawyer didn't want me disappearing back to Mexico.

I wasn't going anywhere. I was going to stay put and pay what was expected of me, but a lot of my clients were based in Mexico, and now I couldn't travel to their offices anymore. A big part of how I could make money was cut off from me. It was a potential disaster.

But there was another thing going on with me.

I was embarrassed. I was ashamed. I had messed up my life. My wife was divorcing me. I couldn't see my kids. I was struggling to pay the legal fees that went with the divorce. I had to find the money to support my wife and kids and keep a roof over their heads. My business partner had taken the money and disappeared. The Great Recession was just beginning, but the credit crunch was already in full swing. The business seemed to be collapsing under my feet, and I couldn't leave the US to visit my clients in Mexico, who represented an important slice of the business.

I made a promise to myself that, whatever happened, I would find the money to support my kids, because my mistakes or failures were not their fault. I had to support them and my ex-wife. That was never in question. With business so bad, that meant I would have to cut back on every possible expense.

I made a list of essential expenditures. Whenever I made any money, I would have to put a significant portion aside for the kids and the alimony payment. I would have to keep a roof over my own head. I would have to pay the essential bills for myself and for the business. Everything else, including food, was non-essential. If I didn't have any money, I wouldn't eat. And if I could afford to spend a bit of money on food, it was going to be the cheapest food there was. If that meant I had to live on tinned tuna and drink nothing but water for a year, that was how it would have to be.

And that's exactly what I did. I lived off tinned tuna. Tuna sandwich; tinned tuna on *pico de gallo*; tinned tuna and pasta. Sometimes I just ate the tuna straight out the tin, with maybe a raw tomato for extra vitamins.

I had to find a way to keep the business going, even though I couldn't leave the country. I wondered if maybe I could have virtual meetings with my international clients and run virtual training meetings for their teams. Remember, we're talking about 2008. The idea of virtual meetings was not common at that time. The technology was there, but it wasn't widely adopted. Zoom wasn't founded until 2011. There was Skype – remember Skype?! – and then there was Webex and Microsoft Live Meeting and some high-end corporate solutions. It was possible to have a virtual meeting, but it wasn't something people in smaller organizations were used to doing or set up for.

But I was still struggling with the other thing: the shame and embarrassment. It would have been very possible for me to abandon the business and get another job. Just put my resume out there and hopefully get a decent, well-paid position and put my head down and earn my way out of my financial problems. I could call my clients or send a general email and say, "Thank you for all the years of doing business together and for all your support, but I have this interesting new opportunity, and I am going to go down this exciting new avenue in my life. Thanks again and goodbye!"

There was a huge temptation to do that, because it wouldn't be a lie. And my clients – people I'd got to know well over the years, many of whom I considered friends – wouldn't have to know how badly I had failed. I could say, "I've got this exciting new opportunity so, sadly, we can't do business together anymore, but thanks. Let's try and catch up sometime soon." There would be no real shame in that. The alternative was having to say, "I fouled up, big time. And now I'm struggling. I'm living in a rented apartment with a few sticks of furniture, struggling to pay the bills and eating tuna out the tin. More importantly, I can't come to see you at your offices in Mexico, because I can't leave the United States due to the legal situation I'm in."

That was the conversation I didn't want to have.

On the other hand, I really loved the business I had built and loved my work with my clients. There was a big emotional connection with my vision – knowing that I was creating something bigger in my life. Something that genuinely helped people build better, stronger businesses of their own. Getting a new job would be about survival. Do the job, get paid, survive. Keeping the business going would be about building on that dream of creating something bigger than me. I could either learn and grow and say, "This should never have happened and mustn't happen again. This is what cuts the line and I need to re-set to zero and build everything all over again." Or, I could just move quietly on, with no one needing to know how badly I had fouled up. But I couldn't hold on to the dream without being honest with my clients. Without saying, "I've messed up big time; I have some problems that mean we have to make new arrangements to keep working together. Can you live with that?"

It wasn't easy to make the decision, and it took me a while. In the meantime, I was just subsisting; scraping by. Eating tuna out the tin because I had to prioritize my spending so I could meet my commitments to my family and pay my legal bills. It was a very difficult time for me. A very dark time.

Finally, I made up my mind. I had built a business I believed was important. Something that was bigger and more important than me as a person. Something that was helping make people's businesses more successful and making a better life for everyone who worked for those businesses.

I think the breakthrough moment was when I thought to myself, "Well, OK, how much worse can it get? Life is terrible. I've lost my wife, my kids, my money, my house. Here I am, staying in a rented apartment with four pieces of furniture, living off tuna, trying to pay my bills and meet my obligations. Can it get any worse?" I decided it couldn't get any worse. This was the bottom.

So how could I climb out?

Logic told me that if I didn't tell my clients anything about my personal situation, I would lose them. It wouldn't make sense to say, "I can't come to your offices in Mexico anymore" without explaining why not. My emotions were telling me to just find a job and walk away.

But then logic reminded me that if I plucked up my courage and told my clients everything, then at least they would have a clear choice to make. They would know everything and be able to make their decision. And I might retain some of them.

I finally made up my mind.

I started to make phone calls to my clients, one by one. They were all incredibly supportive. I couldn't believe what I was hearing. The first thing they'd say would be, "Oh, if you can't come to us, should we send our people to Kansas City so they can get trained? And when we need to talk, can the two of us maybe meet up in Houston?"

But the reaction I got from them was not just a question of, "OK, never mind, let's keep working together." It was an emotional connection of, "You've been completely up-front. You're learning from your mistakes. You're learning from your failures. You're learning from the shame of saying, 'I fucked up. I didn't mean to fuck up, but I did. Now I need to do something to get back on my feet.'" And they were saying, "We really appreciate your honesty. If you're not giving up on us, we're not going to give up on you. We're not going to let anything like that come between us."

It was a big moment for me. It meant a lot.

So now, OK, my clients are maybe prepared to stick with me, for which I'm hugely grateful. Now, how do we make this work?

I have to start doing more video conferences instead of flying to the offices of my clients in Mexico. I have to change my fee structure for remote meetings. I used to charge a daily fee when I was travelling to see clients, and that was generally accepted. "It's taken you a whole day to travel here, talk to us and get home again, so we'll pay your daily rate." But it wasn't fair to charge for a whole day when we were having a virtual meeting and I didn't have to leave the office. I decided I should charge an hourly fee for meetings. But then I worried that clients might feel that wasn't fair either. What if the meeting only lasted half an hour — should I still charge for the whole hour? I started charging by the minute. "That call was 37 minutes long, so here's my fee for 37 minutes." My clients appreciated the transparency.

We began to work together with virtual meetings, which was unprecedented for most people at the time. But I started to prove to everyone that the sessions could work and be just as effective as face-to-face meetings. Nothing is ever quite as good as sitting down together in person, but just as COVID got us all used to virtual meetings, and realizing they worked and could be very effective, so my clients and their teams began to realize, in 2008/09, that I could coach and advise them very effectively via a virtual call.

I was able to keep doing business with my clients in Mexico. The shock of the financial crash receded, and various government schemes to help the economy recover began to take effect. Business began to get back to normal.

To get through this kind of hard time, you need a vision to inspire you and keep you going. If you don't have some kind of vision for the future, you give in to despair. You decide there's nothing you can do about anything, and you might as well go out and spend money you don't have on some nice food or some treat to make you feel better. And then, when the bills come in and you can't pay them, things start to go very bad. But if you have a vision for the future, you can hold on to that vision and it gives you the strength to do everything you can to bring that vision forward. It gives you the strength to do whatever is necessary so you can make that vision of the future real.

To be able to move forward effectively, the first thing you have to do is accept that you're in a hole. You have to understand that logically, and admit to yourself, emotionally, how down you are. Then you can ask the question, like I did, "OK, how much worse can it get?" And when you think, "It can't get any worse," then you can say to yourself, "Do I like really being here or can I move forward?" And the moment you make that connection, it allows you to make that all-important first move forward.

During the first years of losing contact with my kids, every decision I made was based on the assumption that I could get them back the next week, or the next month, or the next year. And there came a day when I realized the reality was that I didn't know when they were going to be back. They were going to be back when they were going to be back. Should I keep making every decision around that one thing, or should I accept it emotionally and just live with it? When you can connect the emotion and the logic in that way, you start moving faster. You still have your vision of the future – one day I will be back on my feet, and I will see the kids again – but you stop making every decision based on the negative thing, the thing you feel worst about.

I was watching a football game with my partner's young son the other day, and there was a particular play that our team made that didn't result in a score, and he said, "We shouldn't use that play again because we're going to fail. We already failed two times." And I said, "OK, but the team made ten great moves before that, and they were so close to scoring. You're focusing on the failures; you're not focusing on the possibility of success."

When we fail at something, we tend to stay focused on the failure. We think, "I know what's going to happen, this is going to fail again, like it did last time." And that stops us from trying again. We don't move forward, because we are still attaching our emotions to the failure instead of attaching our emotions to the success. It's human nature to want to be protected, to be safe, so we focus more on what didn't work instead of what did work. But we need to connect emotionally to what we *can* do – to remind ourselves of all the things we are good at doing – and then to understand logically why something didn't work on a previous occasion.

A lot of people have a business failure, for example, and then think, "I can't try that idea again because it didn't work last time." And I ask, "Well, why did it fail?" And they can always tell me: "Oh, well, this happened, and that happened and then it all went wrong." And I say, "OK, so next time you're not going to do this thing, and you're going to make sure that other thing doesn't happen. You've learned that's what not to do. So this time, that failure won't happen." We have to focus on the possibility of success and not let our experience of the failure we once had stop us from trying again. We need to accept the failure and, in a way, the shame. We all hate to fail. We're ashamed when we fail. But we need to accept what is negative in life as something we can potentially grow from.

My own worst hard times lasted for maybe a year. A year of eating tuna from the tin. With every bit of money I earned, I paid the child support, I paid the alimony and I paid the bills. And then I got to eat, but mainly tuna out the tin. My approach was: I'm not going to have any of the things I may like but are not essential. I don't have dreams at this point other than the dream that I need to get out of this hole."

That pushed me into making these decisions, and I can see today they were the right decisions. But when you're eating tuna every day, after the first month, you start questioning yourself. "Is this the right thing to do? Is it worth it?" You have to step back and tell yourself it's going to work; it's going to be OK. And you will find there is a lot of support out there. The moment that you open up to people and say, "I'm in trouble; I'm in a hole," you find people will support you. Your closest friends, maybe (but not always ...) but also many others who know you; people you have worked with; people you didn't expect to help you. They will say, "We see that you're in a hole, and we're going to get you out of it." And you have to allow them to help you.

It's OK to be vulnerable. It's OK to say, "I'm not OK." And it's OK to be open for people to help you. When you do that and allow life to happen, instead of trying to control life, I think that's when you start to recover. I could have tried to control events and told people I'd just found a new opportunity and wanted to move on, and that would have been easier for me, emotionally. But I would have lost my business, because I couldn't keep it without opening up and telling people how I had made big mistakes in my life, and now I was in a bad place. But once you do that – once you open up and allow people to help you – then every single success that you have is a bonus and a step on the way forward.

I decided that, at the end of each week, if I had made a step forward, I would reward myself with a chocolate, because I love chocolate. So, if there was a good week, I'd go buy a chocolate and enjoy it on the weekend, because that was a small treat I could afford.

I recommend something similar when you're struggling with difficult times. When you have a success, no matter how small, reward yourself with something affordable. Indulge yourself just a little bit. It helps.

Eating tuna straight from the tin wasn't just about the financial hardship; it was a symbol of the sacrifices I had to make. In moments like those, it's easy to feel defeated, as though life has stripped away all the comforts and progress you've worked so hard for. Yet, it was in those moments, sitting with a tin of tuna, that I held on tightly to one thing: my *why*.

The words of philosopher Friedrich Nietzsche, "He who has a why to live for can bear almost any how," resonated deeply during this time. My *why* wasn't grand or lofty – it was simple and clear. I knew what I needed to accomplish, and I knew this phase was temporary. There's a kind of clarity that comes when everything else is stripped away. With no distractions, no fluff, you're left with the bare truth of what drives you.

I think back to Carlos Ruiz Zafón's novel, *La Sombra del Viento* (The Shadow of the Wind), and the way life threw tragedy, mystery and relentless puzzles at the hero, Julian. For Julian, as for me, the journey wasn't just about enduring; it was about finding light in the darkest corners. Every challenge was a step closer to understanding, every setback an opportunity to regroup and redefine what mattered most.

During this time, I found myself living in the present – not in the 'mindful' sense that's trending in pop-culture now, but out of sheer necessity. Each day was its own mountain to climb. I didn't have the luxury of planning far ahead; I had to focus on what I could control in the here and now. Short-term goals became my lifeline. I'd ask myself, "What can I do today to get one step closer? What small win can I create this week?"

This kind of focus required discipline, but it also gave me freedom. I couldn't afford to let myself be overwhelmed by the bigger picture, so I broke it down into manageable pieces. In hindsight, this approach echoed the ideas of Harvard Business School professor John Kotter's work on leading change. Change isn't just about having a vision or even about creating momentum; it's about building a step-by-step process that leads to sustainable transformation. In my case, I wasn't just leading a change in my circumstances, I was leading change within myself.

Kotter talks about the importance of early wins in any transformation. For me, those wins were small but significant: securing a new opportunity, connecting with someone who believed in me, even just finding the strength to keep pushing forward. Each of those wins built my confidence and reinforced my belief that this chapter, difficult as it was, was shaping me for the better.

I also leaned heavily on my narrative, the story I was telling myself. It would have been easy to spiral into self-pity, to see myself as a victim of circumstances. But I chose a different story. I framed this period as a test of my resilience, a necessary part of my growth. I reminded myself that every setback was preparing me for a stronger comeback.

This narrative wasn't just about hope – it was about truth. The truth that life, like any great novel, is full of twists and turns, but the light at the end isn't just a possibility ... it's inevitable if you keep moving forward. Julian's story in *La Sombra del Viento* taught me that, and so did my own experiences.

Looking back, eating tuna out of the tin wasn't a mark of failure. It was a mark of perseverance. It was a reminder that, no matter how difficult the *how* gets, the *why* will always pull you through.

To anyone facing their own tuna-tin moment, I'd offer this:

1. **Keep Your *Why* in Sight**
   When the *how* feels unbearable, let your *why* be your guide. It's the anchor that will keep you grounded.

2. **Focus on Small Wins**
   Don't get overwhelmed by the big picture. Break it down into incremental daily actions and celebrate every step forward.

3. **Embrace the Narrative**
   You're not just living a life; you're telling a story. Make it a story of resilience, courage and transformation.

4. **Trust the Process**
   As Kotter's work on change shows, transformation doesn't happen overnight. It's a series of steps, and each step, no matter how small, matters.

Life's darkest chapters often carry the seeds of our greatest growth. Eating tuna from the tin wasn't glamorous, but it taught me what I'm capable of enduring, and that, no matter how difficult the journey, the light is always waiting at the end of the tunnel. The question is: will you keep walking toward it?

CHAPTER 10

STARTING OVER

The divorce finally came through, and it had not been pretty. Any divorce is difficult and painful. It created a distance between my children and me for many years. But once we had agreed to a divorce settlement and levels of alimony and child support, I set out to rebuild my business so those payments would never fail. I had been forced to let go of my colleagues, my executive coaches, and I became a pioneer in video coaching. I set to work, building up a new business on my own, calling up new clients and delivering a service by myself, with just my assistant, who, as I say, has been with me every single step of the way. And we started again from scratch; we went back to basics. "How do we create money? What has worked for us in the past? Let's get down to logic. Let's get down to basics. Let's create a strong vision, and visualize where we need to go, who we need to be. Let's visualize once again who and what Mau Espinosa is."

And we decided that we sell knowledge. We sell analysis. We sell credibility. This last part has been the core for me ever since: we need, most of all, to be credible. All of that was the logical part.

What about the emotion needed to move forward?

I had already discovered that being 'credible' also had a big emotional aspect to it. You can't be credible without being honest and authentic. That means you have to be prepared to be open with people when things are bad, and when you're ashamed of what you've got yourself into. I also learned that, because the emotional side of things was all down to me, it didn't matter if I was sad; it didn't matter if I was happy; it didn't matter if I was hurting. That had nothing to do with success. Success was all about getting ahead of the game, which meant putting all these emotions to one side.

At that point, I began to understand the importance of mindset vs. emotional state. If my mind was where it needed it to be, my emotions became secondary. I could control my emotions by having a strong mindset. And whatever emotions I was feeling, I had a very strong mindset toward getting back on my feet. I was committed to building up my business all over again, getting my finances back on track and continuing to support my family.

Most important of all, I had to once again become the person I had set out to be.

I started working with that strong mindset and we began to see the results. Month after month, we were paying all the company bills. I was paying my rent, and I was paying child support and alimony. There was a lot of tightening of the belt, cutting back on every possible expense. There was a lot of tinned tuna. It was a hard time that I had to go through, but I did it. Why? Because failure, like success, is never permanent unless you allow it to be. If you stop working on your success, you will lose it. If you don't learn from your failures and move forward, you will remain stuck in them.

That was when I really started to think about change in a more profound way. About how businesses and people have to change in response to changes in market factors and crashes and all the other things that can happen. I began to think about how we have to change in our own lives. It took me another ten years to finally sign up for the Master's degree program in Change Leadership at Oxford University and HEC in Paris in 2018. Two and a half years of studying with the best of the best – not just because of the quality of the schools themselves, but because of your peers, your mentors, your professors – everything associated with those institutions encourages you to study as hard as you can. To discuss and debate things with these brilliant people and really comprehend how to connect your studies to the real world of business and to your own life.

Looking back on all of that, I see now that my response to the outbreak of COVID was like the culmination of everything I had learned up until that point. I knew in 2020 that I had to react fast, because in 2008 I had lost 60% of my income at a time when my expenses had doubled. I knew I had to do something on that day in 2020, that fateful Sunday. I couldn't wait for Monday. I had to give my clients the support this group could offer them, what they needed right then, to make them feel there was a way forward, and that we could get through this together.

That Sunday was like the pinnacle of my understanding of my emotions and how to control them, and how to put the right mindset to work. The mindset was that I knew I could provide a platform for success for my clients. I didn't know exactly how, because nobody knew exactly what we were facing, but my mindset was: I know I can provide this. I have the knowledge to do it. Now, I have to make tactical decisions.

Virtual meetings were far more common by 2020, so I could start having video conferences right away. I knew I could create a narrative. I knew I could create smart, viable solutions for people's businesses once it became clear what we were facing. I worked for the next 48 hours without sleeping, sending out messages, creating something that was tremendously important, because my life and the lives of the people who were now working at my company – I had been able to staff up again after the near meltdown of 2008 – depended on it.

I have told you this story about my emotions and about understanding the logic of life, the logic of personal and business decisions and the tactical decisions we make to deal with life as best we can, because I hope it can serve as a useful illustration and maybe even an inspiration.

Life is not perfect. We are not perfect. We make many mistakes that we'll later regret, and those mistakes can lead us to good decisions or bad decisions in the future. Everything has a positive part and a negative part. I like to focus on the positive part. I can get something positive out of virtually everything, from the losses of my early life to the last big loss of my life, my father, who was probably my biggest fan. He died in 2018, two years before COVID, so he was not able to see me graduate with my Master's degree. My final days with him gave me a new connection to his history as a father, and to my understanding of my own history and my own place in life.

I want to finish this chapter with an event from the middle of the story of my life to date. I believe it was 1998, because we hadn't yet moved to Florida, but I had adopted my daughter, Paige, my ex-wife's child. As Christmas approached, my daughter told me that she hoped Santa Claus would bring her a Barbie House for Christmas.

I was maybe 29 years old. I had come to the US and had managed to get myself promoted to executive coach with my new company, and I was delivering good results. I was excited. My self-esteem as a professional was growing. When my daughter said she wanted a Barbie House, I thought, "Sure, no problem. How much can a house like that cost? $70? $80? Of course I can do that."

At the time, I was very casual about money. I was making what felt like a good income, but I was also spending freely, without any real planning or forethought. Life was good. Money is coming in; let's live a little! And when December came, I suddenly discovered I did not have $70 or $80 in my account, or as credit on any of my cards. I just had $10, and I bought my daughter a Barbie. I didn't buy a Barbie House, I bought a Barbie doll. And she was extremely happy with that doll, but I was in a corner, crying, feeling that I had failed as a father. I had only just become a father for the first time, by adoption, and, already, I had failed.

This became the beginning of the **Life Plans** I talked about earlier, because when you start making money and you start spending money, and making bad decisions about your money, you can end up broke. Maybe not 'out on the streets' broke, but broke enough to not be able to afford some of the really important things in life. Like a Barbie House.

It was hard. But that day, I made a decision that became a mantra for the rest of my life, which is '*Never Again*.' This will never happen again. And I began to understand the power of that mindset, once I'd said to myself, "Never Again."

I told myself that I need to create a budget. I need to create a logical system. I know how much money I make, but I don't know how much money I spend. So, I need to define my silos. What are my obligations, what are my likes, what are my desires, what are my dreams? And that became the beginning of the Life Plans, and the beginning of a mindset focused on never making the same mistakes again. Of course, I made new mistakes. I made the mistakes that led to my divorce, and to losing touch with my kids for many years. But I didn't make the same mistakes. And I had learned about the power of budgeting: of putting money into mental silos, and telling yourself, "That money is not available to you; that money is for the kids/rent/bills," or whatever it might be needed for that is absolutely essential. It's a simple trick, but it works.

To win any race, you must first find the starting line. It doesn't matter how clearly you see the finish line or how perfectly you've mapped out the course. If you don't know where you're starting from, the race might as well be impossible. 'Starting over' is that moment. It's the act of stepping up to the line, of deciding this is where I begin again, of turning preparation into action.

There's a comfort in preparation, in planning and perfecting, but there comes a time when you have to leave the safety of those plans behind and start running. The preparation, the lessons learned, the falls, the resilience – they all lead to this moment. Starting over isn't just about survival; it's about committing to live the life you've dreamed of, to build it with your own hands. It's the decision to stop waiting for the perfect time and realize that now is the only time you have.

For me, starting over meant taking control of my life in a way I never had before. It wasn't just about financial stability or personal satisfaction. It was about carving out a life of intention. I had to stop being a passive observer of my own story and start being its architect. I began creating the framework that would hold my life together, and it all started with defining what success meant for me.

My definition of success wasn't tied to anyone else's standards. It wasn't about a title, a paycheck, or even recognition. Success, for me, was the ability to wake up every morning knowing I was living in alignment with my values, that I was building something meaningful. It was about creating a financial life plan that accounted not just for obligations, but for dreams and desires too. It was about making the deliberate choice to invest in *me*.

That choice became the mantra I've shared with you: *Never Again*. Never again would I let external circumstances define my worth. Never again would I let fear stop me from pursuing my vision. Never again would I sacrifice my future self for temporary comfort. It wasn't just a phrase; it was a commitment – to my growth, to my vision and to the person I was becoming.

This commitment wasn't easy, and it wasn't glamorous. It required discipline – daily, unwavering discipline. Discipline isn't about perfection; it's about persistence. It's about showing up even when you don't feel like it and putting in the work when no one's watching. Discipline is what turns desire into action, and action into results.

But discipline alone isn't enough. It has to be paired with vision. My vision became my compass, guiding me through the uncertainty of starting over. Without a clear vision, it's easy to get lost in the chaos, to let the noise of the world drown out the voice inside you that knows where you're meant to go. My vision wasn't just about the end goal, it was about the journey, About the person I was becoming with every step I took.

And then there was commitment. Commitment is the bridge between vision and discipline. It's the promise you make to yourself that you'll keep going, no matter what. For me, that promise was rooted in a **Real Desire for Success**. Not just a wish or a hope, but a deep, burning desire.

Here's something I often say in my speeches: If your desire doesn't burn you and scare you at the same time, it lacks power and truth. Desire should push you to your limits and pull you toward something greater. It should ignite a fire in you that's impossible to ignore and feels almost too big to contain.

Starting over taught me that success isn't a straight line. It's a series of starts and restarts, of falling down and getting back up.

It's about creating a framework that allows you to adapt and grow while staying true to your vision. For me, that framework was my life plan – a plan that accounted for every silo of my life, from obligations to dreams. It wasn't about balancing them perfectly; it was about ensuring they all had a place in my life.

When you commit to starting over, you're not just choosing to run the race. You're choosing to live. You're choosing to leave behind the safety of preparation and step into the unknown, fueled by the knowledge that every step forward is a step closer to your vision. Starting over isn't the end of the story; it's the beginning of the masterpiece you're carving out of your life.

To anyone standing at the starting line of their own race, I'd say this:

1. **Define Your Success**
   Don't let anyone else dictate what success means for you. Take the time to create a vision that aligns with your values and aspirations.

2. **Commit to Yourself**
   Make a promise to your future self and honor it. Let your why be stronger than your excuses.

3. **Embrace Discipline**
   Show up for yourself every day, even when it's hard. Discipline is the foundation on which success is built.

4. **Start Running**
   Don't wait for the perfect time or the perfect plan. The race starts now, and the only way to win is to begin.

Starting over isn't just a chapter in the story of your life – it's the moment you decide to become the author of your destiny.

THE LIFE PLAN: INTEGRATING L.E.T. (LOGIC, EMOTION, TACTICS)

The essence of human existence lies in the pursuit of purpose, a journey that propels us to discover and follow the path toward our deepest and most meaningful dreams. This journey, at its core, is fuelled by the L.E.T. trio of powerful forces – Logical, Emotional and Tactical pillars that underpin effective leadership across all areas of life. Although we sometimes find ourselves adrift, and facing life's uncertainties without a clear direction, it is here that the **Logical** dimension becomes essential. A life plan, grounded in logical analysis, acts as the beacon that guides us, illuminating our path toward personal achievement and financial security.

The ability to imagine, to dream about what could be, lies at the heart of our human nature. From childhood, our imagination leads us to envision grand achievements, without limits or barriers. This power of visualization is the essence of the **Emotional** dimension of L.E.T. However, as we grow, we face disappointments and what some call the 'realities' of life, which tend to condition and limit our thoughts and aspirations. It's crucial to recognize that such so-called realities and limitations are mere illusions. With a life plan that embraces both logic and emotion, we can rekindle those youthful visions and turn them into a map charting the way to our dream destinations.

This life plan is not merely a set of goals; it is a **Tactical** strategy, a roadmap designed to take us from where we are to where we wish to be. Unlike ephemeral goals, it offers a strategic approach that immerses us in an exciting journey toward the fulfillment of our dreams. Here, the Tactical dimension manifests itself, providing the concrete actions and detailed steps necessary for personal and professional realization.

THE FINANCIAL FRAMEWORK: FOUR SILOS OF SPENDING

A life plan must include a financial roadmap. Managing our finances effectively means dividing expenditures into four key categories: **Obligations**, **Likes**, **Desires** and **Dreams**. Each silo represents a critical aspect of financial discipline and contributes to creating a life of balance and purpose.

1. OBLIGATIONS: WHAT WE MUST PAY

Obligations are the non-negotiable financial commitments that form the foundation of our expenditures. These include rent or mortgage payments, debt repayments, utilities, insurance premiums and other fixed or recurring expenses. Obligations represent the baseline costs that must be met before other financial goals can be pursued.

- **Recommended Allocation:** 50–60% of income.
- **Key Actions:**
  - List all recurring expenses and categorize them as fixed or variable.
  - Set a benchmark percentage of your income to manage obligations effectively.
  - Automate payments to avoid penalties and stay consistent.

2. LIKES: THE SMALL JOYS OF LIFE

Likes are the small indulgences that bring us happiness without breaking the bank. These are things like a special chocolate bar, coffee at your favorite cafe, a family trip to the zoo, a movie night, or catching a local football game. While they may seem minor, these moments contribute to emotional wellbeing.

- **Recommended Allocation:** 5–10% of income.
- **Key Actions:**
  - Plan Likes intentionally to avoid overspending.
  - Use a monthly budget to track these smaller expenditures.
  - Embrace rituals, such as a weekly coffee or monthly outing, to make them meaningful.

3. DESIRES: MEDIUM-TERM GOALS

Desires require some planning and effort but are achievable in the near future. These include experiences like a weekend getaway, attending a concert in another city or purchasing a home appliance.

- **Recommended Allocation:** 10–15% of income.
- **Key Actions:**
  - Prioritize Desires by creating a ranked list.
  - Use dedicated savings accounts to fund these goals.
  - Plan within a 6–12-month window to maintain focus and momentum.

4. DREAMS: LONG-TERM ASPIRATIONS

Dreams are the ambitious goals that define our deepest desires, such as becoming debt-free, travelling to Paris, buying a dream home or retiring early. Achieving Dreams requires significant time, effort and financial planning.

- **Recommended Allocation:** 10–20% of income.
- **Key Actions:**
  - Define each Dream clearly, with timelines and financial milestones.
  - Break down Dreams into smaller, actionable steps.
  - Stay disciplined by tracking your progress toward your Dreams.

MAINTAINING FINANCIAL STABILITY: PLANNING AS THE FOUNDATION

Balancing these four silos requires discipline, planning and awareness. Without a plan, it's easy to overspend on Likes, leaving no room for Desires and Dreams.

THE CORE LESSONS

1. **Awareness is Essential**
   Understand where your money is going.

2. **Discipline Drives Results**
   Consistency is key to achieving goals.

3. **Small Wins Build Momentum**
   Weekly progress tracking keeps motivation high.

4. **Planning Turns Dreams Into Reality**
   A structured plan bridges the gap between aspiration and achievement.

DESIGNING YOUR LIFE PLAN

A life plan is a dance between Logic, Emotion and Tactics. It is the art of shaping our aspirations, integrating our deepest desires with strategic focus and unbreakable determination. By managing Obligations, indulging in Likes, planning for Desires and pursuing Dreams, we create a fulfilling and purposeful life.

The power of L.E.T. resides within you. It is the engine that drives your journey toward personal discovery, the realization of dreams and the building of a lasting legacy. Design your life plan today, reflect your true essence and embark on the journey toward your unlimited potential.

I'd like to introduce you to a special tool that will help you to focus on your personal strategies and measure how you're progressing toward achieving your goals.

It's called the **Triumphometer**.

The Triumphometer is a powerful device of my own invention that's designed to measure progress toward achieving desires and dreams, as defined within the broader framework of a Life Plan. These goals often fall into the medium- or long-term categories, requiring discipline, motivation and strategic focus to bring them to life. The Triumphometer helps transform aspirations into actionable steps by breaking down their financial requirements into manageable milestones.

Ideally, the Triumphometer will have some physical form, like a calendar or a spreadsheet. You can keep track of these incremental steps in your head, but I'm sure you'll find it is much more effective if there's something you can physically see, at a glance, that shows your progress toward your chosen goals.

At its core, the Triumphometer bridges the gap between ambition and achievement. It helps you:

1. **Identify your goals (desires and dreams).**

2. **Calculate their financial costs.**

3. **Translate these costs into achievable, periodic targets (weekly or monthly).**

4. **Track your progress with measurable actions and outcomes.**

Whether your income is fixed or variable, this tool helps create a clear and motivating pathway to financial success. For individuals with variable incomes, such as sales professionals, the Triumphometer is particularly impactful, as it ties additional efforts directly to tangible outcomes.

The **Weekly Triumphometer** is a practical and motivational tool designed to help individuals align their weekly actions with their long-term desires and dreams. It integrates a clear timeline with checkpoints for accountability, providing a structured framework for monitoring progress toward specific goals.

This system ensures that every week counts by emphasizing reflection, planning and execution. It keeps users focused on their goals, promotes disciplined action and enables course correction if necessary.

HOW IT WORKS

- **Goal Setting**
  At the beginning of the timeline (a month, quarter or year), the user defines a **desire** (a family vacation) or a **dream** (becoming debt-free) along with a realistic target date. The calendar marks the final week as the **Goal Week**, the point by which the desire or dream should be achieved.

- **Weekly Checkpoints**
  Each week is broken into two key actions:
  - **Reflection:** Evaluate whether the necessary actions from the previous week were completed.
  - **Planning:** Outline specific steps to take in the coming week to stay on track.

- **Accountability Markers**
  The calendar includes:
  - A **progress bar** or tracker to visualize the cumulative percentage of the goal achieved.
  - Space for a weekly self-assessment, with prompts like:
    - Did I complete the required actions this week?
    - What obstacles did I encounter, and how will I address them next week?

  - › A section for marking milestones or incremental achievements, such as transferring a certain amount into a 'Dream Savings' account.

- **Midpoint Review**
  Halfway through the timeframe, users perform a deeper reflection:
  - › Are my actions yielding the expected results?
  - › Do I need to adjust my strategies to meet my target?

- **Final Weeks' Push**
  As the **Goal Week** approaches, the calendar prompts intensify in focus, encouraging users to accelerate efforts to close any gaps between their progress and their goal.

FEATURES OF THE WEEKLY TRIUMPH CALENDAR

- **Visual Goal Tracker**
  A section of the calendar visually represents progress toward the goal, offering constant motivation.

- **Reflection Prompts**
  Weekly prompts encourage introspection and accountability.

- **Customizable Milestones**
  Users can define their own weekly milestones and rewards.

- **Flexible Design**
  The calendar works for both short-term desires and long-term dreams.

EXAMPLE: SAVING FOR A DREAM VACATION

- **Goal:** Save $5,000 for a dream vacation in six months.
- **Weekly Target:** Save $200 per week through extra work or reduced spending.
- **Weekly Actions:** Close one additional client or reduce discretionary spending by $200.

Week 1:

- **Action:** Closed one extra client / saved $300.
- **Reflection:** "Exceeded my goal this week! Motivated to continue."

Week 4:

- **Action:** Had fewer clients / saved $150 instead of $200.
- **Reflection:** "Fell short this week. I'll try to add one additional client next week to make up for it or further reduce my discretionary spend."

Midpoint Review (Week 13):

- **Progress:** Saved $2,800, slightly ahead of schedule.
- **Reflection:** "On track! Need to maintain focus for the remaining weeks."

Final Week:

- **Achieved Goal:** $5,000 saved.
- **Reflection:** "Vacation is booked. Success!"

CHAPTER 11

LOGIC

Now that I've told you a bit about myself, how I came to see the forces of logic and emotion at play in my own life, and realized the power of tactical decisions to help us engage with emotion in a positive way and make effective decisions in life, I'd like to explore the central concept of this book – L.E.T. – more directly.

Let's start with Logic.

The logical elements in our thinking are the rational, structured aspects of decision-making that help us navigate our personal and professional lives. Logical elements in our decision-making include:

- **Goals and Objectives:** Clearly defined outcomes you aim to achieve.
- **Plans and Strategies:** Detailed steps and approaches to reach your goals.
- **Resources and Capabilities:** Identification and utilization of available assets and skills.
- **Analysis and Evaluation:** Assessment of situations and options based on data and evidence.
- **Timelines and Deadlines:** Setting realistic timeframes for achieving milestones.
- **Risk Management:** Identifying potential risks and developing mitigation strategies.
- **Feedback and Adaptation:** Continually assessing progress and making necessary adjustments.

The wonderful thing about logic is that it seems so obvious to us. The parts of our brain that deal with logic, reasoning and decision-making are also, broadly speaking, the parts that give us our sense of identity. We think of ourselves as rational beings, so we're comfortable with logic and find it more difficult to recognize the influence our emotions have on everything we do. (More about that in the next chapter.) We feel comfortable talking about analysis and evaluation, and plans and strategies, because we feel this is what we do all the time – in business, in particular, but also in our personal lives. We see ourselves as setting goals and objectives; analyzing situations and creating strategies and setting deadlines; making contingency plans to deal with problems we might face along the way; getting feedback about our progress and adjusting our plans accordingly. It's all so straightforward and logical, and we tell ourselves that is how we approach every issue in our lives, business or personal.

Except, as we said at the beginning of this book, human beings don't actually work that way.

Let's take a couple of examples from my coaching experience. The first example is a lady called Valentina. She owns a fitness center. Before she owned the business, she was a personal trainer – one of the best in the industry. Now that she is running her own business she is, as you would expect, very focused. She knows what she wants from the business. She has a very logical plan. She has a clear professional goal, which is to be able to grow her business sufficiently to be able to sell it in maybe ten years' time and retire on the proceeds. She has targets and milestones, and she understands the resources she'll need to achieve them. It is all, as I say, very logical. And, because of her background as a personal trainer, she doesn't lack commitment or the willpower; she knows what she wants to achieve, and nothing will get in her way.

But things do keep getting in her way. No matter how hard she tries, she doesn't seem to be able to find trainers to work with her members who share her passion and commitment. She feels that her staff keep letting her down, and she finds this incredibly frustrating.

She feels like her goals are slipping out of her grasp, and there's nothing she can do about it. No matter how hard she works, she can't do everything herself, and the business isn't growing like she knows it could. It's a good gym, but she doesn't seem to be able to make it a great one – the kind she dreams of, that she will be able to sell at a premium price when she is ready.

What Valentina struggles with is the ability to recognize the different levels of emotion her employees bring to her business, and her own emotional reaction to that. She expects everybody to work at the same high level of professionalism and dedication as herself, and she maybe forgets, or doesn't even have a clear understanding of, how exceptional she is: perhaps in the top 3% in her profession.

One of her trainers, for example, is a guy who recently got married. His wife is about to have a baby, and although he's a conscientious worker and he does a good job, his focus right now is more on his wife and the coming baby. Another trainer is more focused on his own success: he knows how he wants his career to develop and where he wants to go next, and he's not so focused on helping Valentina achieve the success she dreams of. There is another trainer, a woman, who idolizes Valentina. She tries to mimic everything her boss does and seems to want to be another Valentina. But this person is still a little business-immature, unsurprisingly, and not able to give Valentina the kind of support Valentina would like. She is always looking to Valentina for advice and guidance, while Valentina would like to have somebody who could work alongside her as more of an equal partner and help ease the strain of running the business.

Everybody is engaging with the company at different levels, according to their own emotional journeys and the personal story of their own lives.

Working with Valentina as a consultant, I suggested she should think of the business as being like a game of chess, where not every piece on the board has the same abilities or powers. She herself was clearly a Queen, able to take on almost every role, and make every move, but not everyone else was a Queen. There are different pieces on the board, and in order to win the game you need to use their individual abilities and powers to best effect.

Valentina struggles with this because she sees the potential in every one of her team. She sees what they could become, and struggles when she sees them not fully engaging and not delivering the full performance she believes they're capable of. Often, she ends up putting too much pressure on people. She will hire someone new and tell me how she loves this person: this is the best person ever; at last, she's found the kind of person she's been looking for! She tells me how great they are and how good it's all going to be. Then, six months later, it's not working so well, and eventually the person leaves and then it's the same story all over again. As a result, the business isn't growing as fast as she planned and expected.

Eventually I was able to tell her, "You have your logical plan, which is perfect. What we're missing are the emotional connection and the tactics. To create the emotional connection, we need to understand everyone's personal life plans. Where do these people want to go? You know where you would like to take them, but those are two different things. The tactics involve demonstrating the link between people's personal life plans and how work can help them achieve what they want in their lives."

Very often, we create a plan for one of our employees, and we can clearly see the path that person can take. But when we talk to them, we find they have a completely different idea of what they want to do. And that's where the emotional disconnection happens. That's a big problem. I hear a lot about a company's professional plans, and I say, "Great! I love the professional plan. But now show me the personal plans. How do they tie together?"

If we don't have the employee's life plan in mind, there's not going to be that essential emotional connection to the business, because everybody works for their own personal gain. As I said earlier, they work *at* the company, but they don't work *for* the company. That can sound like semantics, but, in terms of mindset, it's important to understand. It's different when we understand that people work at the company to create the income that's necessary for what they want to achieve in their lives. The moment we can connect those two things – what people want in their lives and how work is helping them achieve those things – that's when people become fully engaged.

I worked with Valentina on developing a plan that would bring everyone's work and life plan together. That trainer who was very wrapped up in his personal life and his wife and the coming baby – he wasn't going to double down on work anytime soon because the baby would be born, and a lot would change in his life. But, in the meantime, he was completely committed to the job because it was making the money he needed for his family. He'd do a good job but would need a bit of help and understanding, and recognition that he was not going to deliver 110% to the company right now. But maybe later he would, because he'd be grateful for the support and understanding he had been given. And then the person who was ambitious on his own behalf and perhaps not fully committed to the business ... let's work with that. Let's get 110% input from him right now, but with the understanding that he will probably be moving on soon to develop his own career. And maybe the woman who wants to be another Valentina will get there one day, and make a huge contribution, and maybe become Valentina's right-hand person and even her successor. Meanwhile, she would need a lot of help and encouragement and advice, but that would hopefully be a good investment and a good use of Valentina's time and effort.

It was all about recognizing what people were best able to contribute given their current personal stage in life, and leveraging that. Yet, Valentina's instincts and training had her wanting to see everyone performing at 110% of their abilities all the time, just like she did.

Let me offer one more example of the effect of people's emotional states on the logic of our business plans, and how we need to use tactical solutions to encourage people to deliver the best performance they're capable of in their current circumstances.

A manager in a car business I work with was frustrated by one of his salespeople, a young man named Steven. The manager was certain that Steven could sell more cars than he was. He would tell me, "I know he can sell more, but he doesn't want to because he lives with his mom and dad, and he's not motivated to try harder. He sells one car a week and then he feels like he's done his job, when I know he could sell at least two a week, no problem! And I could just let him go, because he's not meeting his targets, but I know he can do this. He has everything he needs to perform much better and it's driving me crazy!" I said, "OK, let's talk to Steven."

Turned out, the life goal for Steven right now was to finish college and then go on to a better job. He saw the car salesroom as a way of earning money to get himself through college and then, with his new degree, he'd be able to move on to a better job. He liked his current job, and he liked the company, and he wanted to do a good job while he was there. It was just that he knew he wouldn't be there for long and wasn't emotionally engaged.

I asked the manager, "So why are you trying to get him to do all these things while his mind is set on something else? What if we work with him and understand what he wants in order to go on to a better job after he finishes college? Why don't we find out what this 'better job' looks like for him?"

We talked to Steven, and he was very straightforward and forthcoming. He told us his idea of the "better job" would be with a big-name corporation. He was hoping to get an entry-level position and then work his way up, because what he was studying was going to help him land the job and then help him progress in his new career. He saw his future self as an executive more than a salesperson.

I said, "OK, so these companies, what do they ask from you? What are the requirements you need to get accepted by them?"

He started telling us the requirements, and one of them was two years' experience at another company. I said, "OK. We can give you the experience, and, at the end of those two years, we can give you the best letter of recommendation anyone can have. Any big-name company is going to read that letter and think, 'This is the guy for us! We have to get him onboard!' But to get that perfect referral, you're going to have to achieve some goals that we're going to set for you. And we're going to help you achieve those goals, because we think you have what it takes to do this. We think you can be great at this job! And then, we'll be able to say in our letter of recommendation, 'Steve was with us for two years, and we loved working with him, and he smashed all his targets and we can't recommend him highly enough!'"

Steven is now selling not four, but 14 cars a month, and he's earning excellent commission. He's earning more than four times the commission he used to pull, because there's a sliding scale based on volume. Now, he's comparing the money he's earning to what he could potentially make as an executive, provided everything went well and he managed to work his way up in the company, because the entry-level salary is nowhere near what he's earning now.

In the end, Steven decided to stay with the car business. As he told me after he had made his decision, "They're not going to pay me what I'm earning here for a long time, and I'm achieving everything that I wanted for the future with my career here. So, I'm planning to stay."

The company had made the emotional connection with Steven. It understood what he wanted in his own life, and it had offered him a route to achieving that. The logic of the situation is clear: the company wants to sell more cars. Understanding the emotional aspect from the employee's perspective allows us to use a tactical approach to bring the logic and emotion together. The tactics find a way to engage the emotions of the person, so they can see how their work today is helping them advance into the future they want for themselves and their families.

I can't emphasize enough how important this connection is. If we treat people as if they are inanimate parts of a mechanical process, we can't hope to engage with them emotionally. I remember when I had my first jobs, in Mexico, as I was working through high school and college. This was in the days before pay was deposited directly into people's bank accounts, and you would go to the office of your manager, who would give you an envelope with your earnings for the week. The envelope would contain cash, and you would pull the money out and count it in front of the manager to be sure it was the right amount. While you were doing that, the manager would be giving you feedback. "Hey, that was a good week. You did a really good job on that project, thanks a lot. Next week we have this new assignment coming up and we really need your help on that." Because of this simple ritual of handing over the week's pay, every employee would get several minutes of personal feedback from their manager on a regular basis.

We don't have the same opportunities for that level of feedback in the modern office. We've lost one of the most important tools we have as managers, which is providing feedback on a consistent basis. We have lost that connection. The bigger the company, the worse the problem is. We might have off-site gatherings and retreats, but there's not the same regular, one-on-one feedback that allows us to constantly adjust the tactics we need to ensure that our logical goals and plans and strategies stay aligned with people's day-to-day emotional realities.

The feedback must be specific and personal. Otherwise, it is meaningless, because it doesn't make an emotional connection. It needs to say, "Hey, did you see that? With what you did this month, you were able to provide your family with that thing we talked about months ago that you really wanted. How can we repeat that? Because the challenge for the company next month is ..."

That specific, personal feedback provides the recognition we all crave. Recognition is a prime motivator for all of us, including leaders and company owners. The closer you get to the top of any organization, the less people will feel able to tell you you're doing a great job. They feel it's not their place. If we circle back to Valentina and her fitness center, a lack of support and recognition was at the heart of her insecurity and anxiety. There was no one to say, "You're doing a great job! I can see how difficult it must be. It must be really disappointing when the people you hire don't live up to your expectations, and you feel they're letting themselves down. But, hey, this is a great business! Not every team member can be a superstar like you. You're running things really well!"

One of the great benefits of my line of business – peer group networking – is that when you join such a group, you get affirmation from your peers. You get people saying, "You might want to try this; it worked really well for us." But you will also have your counterparts saying, "Wow, you've done an amazing job. Congratulations!" And that can go a long way toward providing the recognition you need and deserve.

Logic is hugely important in business. Logic supplies the numbers we need to run our company efficiently: you hit your target; you achieved your KPIs. Or you didn't. Any manager these days just has to hit a button and there are the charts, for everyone to see. "We were X% up against this target but Y% down against this one." But the numbers don't motivate people; they don't inspire anyone. (More about motivation and inspiration in the next chapter.) Logic needs to be linked to emotion via tactics. People need feedback to show them how their efforts are helping them achieve something meaningful in their own lives, and they need recognition that they've done a good job.

Logic tells people if they have hit a target or not. The other two aspects – **emotion** and **tactics** – determine whether they have the motivation to turn up for work tomorrow and try again.

The stories of Valentina and her gym and Steven at the car dealership illuminate the role of logic, not just as a framework for setting goals and strategies, but as the foundation for engaging emotions and executing tactics effectively. These examples also reflect broader leadership concepts, such as adaptive leadership, scenario planning and fostering a culture of innovation, all of which are essential to navigating challenges and achieving success.

LOGIC AS A CORE ELEMENT IN ADAPTIVE LEADERSHIP

Adaptive leadership, as outlined by Harvard's Heifetz and Linsky, emphasizes the need to navigate complexity and mobilize people to tackle tough challenges. The stories of Valentina and Steven demonstrate how logic provides a starting point for addressing these challenges. For Valentina, her logical business plan outlined clear goals, milestones and resources. However, the gap between her logical expectations and the emotional realities of her employees revealed the limitations of logic alone. Similarly, Steven's manager approached his performance from a purely logical standpoint, expecting higher sales based on his potential without considering the young man's personal goals and emotional engagement.

The adaptive pivot in both cases involved moving beyond logic to understand the emotional contexts and designing tactics that aligned personal aspirations with organizational objectives. For Valentina, this meant recognizing that her employees were not all 'Queens' on the chessboard. Each had unique strengths and limitations. By tailoring her approach to each individual's emotional journey, she was able to engage them more effectively. This aligns with the adaptive leadership principle of 'getting on the balcony,' which requires leaders to step back, assess the whole system and make adjustments that address both logical and emotional dynamics.

SCENARIO PLANNING: BRIDGING LOGIC AND EMOTION

Scenario planning involves imagining possible futures and preparing strategies to navigate them. Steven's story is a perfect illustration of this concept. When his manager shifted the conversation from immediate sales targets to Steven's long-term career aspirations, they effectively created a shared scenario: his two-year tenure at the company could serve as a launchpad for his future goals. This alignment of scenarios provided Steven with a clear and logical path forward while tapping into his emotional drivers – his ambition and desire for success. The tactical element was establishing performance goals tied to Steven's aspirations, which resulted in his increased engagement and productivity and, ultimately, his staying on with the company.

In both Valentina's and Steven's cases, scenario planning bridged the gap between the logic of the business's goals and the emotional realities of the individuals involved. This approach not only enhanced individual performance but also contributed to a culture of trust and alignment, fostering innovation and collaboration.

THE ROLE OF LOGIC IN CHANGE MANAGEMENT

Change management, particularly as articulated by Harvard's John Kotter, stresses the importance of clear goals, vision and communication. Valentina's initial struggles highlight the challenges of implementing change when logic is not coupled with emotional connection and tactical execution. Her logical plan for growing the business was sound, but without understanding her team's personal goals, she struggled to inspire the level of commitment and performance needed to achieve her vision.

When Valentina began incorporating her employees' personal life plans into her business strategy, she effectively addressed one of Kotter's key principles: creating alignment and engagement through a shared vision. This approach didn't just motivate her team; it also empowered them to contribute to the company's success in ways that resonated with their own life goals.

LOGIC AS A CATALYST FOR INNOVATION

Innovation thrives at the intersection of logic and creativity. Both stories in this chapter underscore the importance of using logic as a foundation for fostering innovative solutions. In Steven's case, the logical framework of his career progression provided a platform for rethinking his role within the company. This led to a win-win situation: Steven exceeded expectations by selling more cars, and the company gained a highly productive and engaged employee.

The chessboard analogy I applied to Valentina's situation highlights how logic can guide creative problem-solving. By understanding her employees' unique contributions and aligning their roles with her business objectives, she was able to reimagine her team's dynamics. This approach mirrors the process of design thinking, where logical frameworks are used to identify problems, and creative strategies are then employed to address them.

Valentina's story reinforces the need for adaptive leadership by showing how logic must be balanced with emotional intelligence to address the complexities of workplace dynamics. Her journey exemplifies scenario planning by illustrating how understanding individual motivations can create pathways for collective success. Similarly, Steven's story demonstrates the principles of change management and the power of aligning personal and organizational goals to drive engagement and innovation.

Both narratives emphasize that logic alone isn't enough. Leaders must embrace the interplay of logic, emotion and tactics to inspire their teams, foster resilience and drive sustainable success. This integration creates a culture where people feel valued and empowered to contribute their best, aligning their personal aspirations with the organization's goals.

In conclusion, logic provides the structure and clarity needed to navigate the complexities of leadership, but it must be complemented by emotional engagement and tactical execution. The stories in this chapter serve as powerful examples of how these elements come together to drive performance, inspire innovation and create meaningful connections that lead to lasting success.

CHAPTER 12

EMOTION

We've seen how logic, emotion and tactics are inextricably linked. There is always a logical aspect to any business decision. Nobody has any success in business doing things that don't make sense; there is always a rationale behind our decisions. The problem is that the logic seems so irrefutable. We devise a plan or a process or a system and it's clear to us that it will deliver the results we want. We plan to do A, then B, then C, so it is inevitable that outcome D will come next, because logic tells us so. Unfortunately, **people don't act on logic, they act on emotion.** They will listen to the logic and fully understand it and agree with every aspect of it: "This is a plan that absolutely will work, one hundred percent." But they don't actually implement the plan, because they are not emotionally engaged. They don't have the internal motivation to put the plan into action.

We see examples of this all the time in our daily lives. We know that we should lose weight, and we fully understand the regimen of diet and exercise that would lead to weight loss. We buy a diet book, we read it, and it's completely convincing. It shows us exactly what we need to do, step by step. Perhaps we actually take the first step, or even the first two steps, but then we stop. We run out of motivation. It's only when something happens that gives us the real impetus to carry out the plan that we start again, and this time we see it through. Maybe there is a big event coming up and we want to be able to wear that suit or that dress and it would be humiliating for us to turn up not looking our best. Or perhaps we have a health scare. Whatever it is that makes us really change our diet and exercise regularly will be some vision of the future that we genuinely want to make a reality. Something that keeps us going and sustains us when we don't feel like going for a run, or we're really hungry and we want to eat that tempting piece of cake.

Sometimes, to make really big changes in our lives, it takes a major life event to give us the motivation to make it so. More often, it's simply being able to visualize some future state that we want to make happen, like walking into the big event and looking good. It's just a simple vision, but it's enough to make the emotional connection between the logic and the emotion that will make us change our behavior.

When we talk about it in these terms, it's obvious. There are many things we 'should' do, and even things that we actually *want* to do, but we don't do them until something gives us real motivation. In business, we tend to forget this. We get blinded by the logic. If we do A, B and C, then we will achieve D, and D is the target: success! But the target doesn't mean anything to the people on our teams unless we've made some emotional connection with them. So they can imagine how it will *feel* to achieve that target, and what it will mean to them personally – that achieving the target will make some small but real difference to their lives.

Leadership is all about leading with emotion. It's about making an emotional connection with people that gives them the real motivation to do the work needed to achieve the greater goal.

Think of it this way: as the use of AI becomes more prevalent in business, it will increasingly be possible to feed a computer program the details of a particular business scenario and ask it to provide the perfect solution. The answer that AI supplies will follow impeccable logic. It will work out the resources needed, design the perfect team structure and even devise a bonus system that would give people a clear financial incentive to carry out the tasks needed to achieve the business goal. It will provide each team member with precise instructions.

Ask yourself this: if you're running a business and AI promised to supply all this, would you hand over the running of the business to AI and head for the beach? Would you be confident your team would feel motivated to carry out the AI plan, and that you wouldn't need you and your managers to be there to make sure the plan was carried out?

I doubt it.

I'm not saying that AI will not be used in business planning. I'm certain it will be applied in this way, and that it will prove to be a valuable tool. What I am saying is that people will not follow a plan they don't feel emotionally invested in, and that we will always need human beings to embody that plan and bring it to life. Even the best, most logical incentive plan is not enough to bring people to work every day. People work for reasons other than money, and those include a sense of belonging to something bigger than themselves, and a sense of taking part in a common effort and contributing to its success. People need a human, emotional connection with a leader. It has to be someone we trust; someone who speaks to us in a way that tells us they care about us and want to help make our lives better in some way. That can be a very simple thing, like feeling good because the team we work for has raised some money for a local charity, or because our organization has won an award that recognizes everyone's efforts and makes us proud to be part of the team.

In my opinion, machines are never going to be able to prioritize according to people. A software program can prioritize in a logical way, based on the information we give it. But let's imagine that someone calls in sick on a particular day, and the machine is tasked with finding someone else to take over their role. How will it cope with the realities of each person's suitability for the task? A human manager might decide, "Amanda could do this work perfectly well, but she's new and she tends to resent being asked to take on anything she feels is outside her job description." Or, "James would be good, but he's having some problems at home and is in a bit of a fragile state at the moment." Or, "Jimenez is a kind of genius, but he's just not good with people. This isn't something he will deal with well."

It's human and it's emotional, and the day that machines are truly capable of dealing with issues like this is the day the machines become, effectively, human. In the meantime, machines may be able to deal with the logic of business, but the need for human beings to handle the emotional aspects of working together and doing business is a reminder of the significance of emotion in the triad of logic, emotion and tactics.

My company runs regular leadership retreats designed to help leaders understand themselves as emotional beings. The retreats also explore the use of storytelling as a way of coming to a better understanding of ourselves, and as a tool to open up a new direction for our lives. We'll talk more about narrative and storytelling later in the book. In this chapter, I want to talk about the early sessions of the three-day retreat, which involve working with horses to help reach a better understanding of ourselves as emotional beings.

Before I tell you about all that, I'd like to draw a distinction between emotions, feeling and sensations.

Emotions are complex psychological states that involve three distinct components: a subjective experience, a physiological response and a behavioral or expressive response. They are often automatic reactions to stimuli, playing a crucial role in survival by prompting quick responses to environmental challenges. A perceived threat may trigger the emotion of fear, leading to a fight-or-flight response. Our bodies produce hormones that increase our heart rate, blood pressure and blood sugar levels and heighten our alertness and focus, getting us ready to respond. Emotions are not inherently good or bad; they simply exist. Their impact on us depends on factors like intensity and duration. Emotions also serve as the glue to memories; significant events are often etched in our minds because of the emotional weight they carry.

Feelings are our conscious experience of emotional reactions. They arise when we become aware of the physical sensations our emotional responses are causing. While emotions can be observed through physiological changes, feelings are personal and subjective, shaped by individual experiences, beliefs and memories. For example, two people might experience the emotion of fear, but their feelings about that fear can differ based on past experiences and personal interpretations.

Sensations are the raw data our bodies receive from the environment through our sensory organs – sight, sound, touch, taste and smell. They're the initial inputs that our nervous system processes.

The warmth of the sun on our skin or the aroma of freshly baked bread are sensations. These sensory inputs can trigger emotions; the scent of a particular perfume might evoke feelings of nostalgia or happiness due to the memories we associate it with.

The relationship between these three elements is dynamic. Sensations can lead to emotions, which in turn give rise to feelings. For instance, touching a hot surface (sensation) can cause pain (emotion), leading to discomfort or distress (feeling). Conversely, our feelings can influence how we perceive sensations. Someone feeling anxious might interpret a neutral sensation, such as a gentle touch, as threatening. The feeling of anxiety may have been triggered by the emotion of fear: a perceived threat has triggered our body's fear response, making us feel especially alert and on edge.

The American psychologist Robert Plutchik developed the concept of a 'Wheel of Emotions' to illustrate the relationships between different emotional states. He identified eight primary human emotions: joy, trust, fear, surprise, sadness, disgust, anger and anticipation. He arranged these in a circle to show opposites: joy vs. sadness; trust vs. disgust; fear vs. anger; surprise vs. anticipation. The emotional states on the outer edge of the wheel reflect increasing intensity – feeing stressed might intensify into feeling overwhelmed or out of control. Plutchik suggests that complex emotions arise from blends of more basic ones, with a combination of joy and trust perhaps giving rise to love.

In our leadership retreats, we work with horses because they act like emotional mirrors. They don't care about our title, our credentials or the carefully crafted version of ourselves we show to the world. They respond to the energy of our emotions – the real ones, not the ones we try to mask. You can't fake it with a horse. If you're anxious, frustrated or unsure, the horse will reflect that right back to you. Horses are also not judgemental; they give you honest feedback in the purest form. It's like having a live emotional barometer walking alongside you. That's what makes them the perfect partners for our retreats.

The retreats I mentioned take place on a ranch where we have a herd of horses. I say a 'herd' because we don't ride these horses or ask them to do any work. They live together as a herd, and they interact with each other in a natural way. They are all rescue horses we have taken on because they're too old to do whatever they used to do for their owners, or perhaps they were sick and we nurse them back to health, or 'difficult' ones that people found hard to ride or train to do work. So, they're used to being around humans, but once they come to us , they live as a herd, in the open. They don't live in stables, although we have stables to bring them to if they need one. They live as horses have always lived, before humans started to use them as a means of transportation or for their muscle power. At any one time, we have between five and nine horses.

When leaders come to the ranch, we get them to interact with the horses and undertake various activities with them. One of the first things we ask them to do is to take a rope, put it round a horse's neck and lead it back to the group. Spoiler alert: it's not as easy as it sounds. Maybe the horse hesitates, or it refuses to follow you. You feel a flood of sensations – your heart races, your palms sweat, your chest tightens. Those are sensations, the physical cues your body gives you. Next, you feel the emotional response: maybe frustration, maybe fear. And then come the feelings: "I can't do this," or "I'm not good enough."

This is where the work begins. Over the three days of the retreat, we help leaders break this down. They learn to identify their sensations, separate them from their emotions and untangle the stories their feelings are telling them. Most importantly, they learn to channel their emotions into purposeful, intentional action.

The key thing about horses is that they react to emotions, not words (and certainly not to logic). No matter how you talk to them, they react only to emotion. You can talk to a horse in in English, in Spanish, in German, in Chinese – it makes no difference. The horse doesn't understand anything you say. It responds only to emotions. Horses, big as they are, are animals of prey. They are herbivores, so they don't attack any other animals, but they can be attacked by large predators. In times past they fell prey to wolves, sabretooth tigers and other big cats, for example. A horse's genes tell it to be always alert to danger. If you run toward a horse or approach it in a threatening way, it will move away, slowly at first, and faster if it feels really threatened. A horse will let you approach if it doesn't feel threated, but it will only *follow* you if it feels it has an emotional connection with you and can trust you.

When people who aren't used to working with horses first approach the horse, they tend to assume that the horses are like people. That you can talk to them, maybe cajole them, perhaps even command them and tell them what to do. We are the humans, after all. The assumption is that we have 'mastered' horses, so we should be masterful and tell them what to do.

It doesn't work.

There's a true story about myself that I often tell people at these retreats. I was on a four-hour flight from Mexico City to Chicago. I got on board, put my luggage in the overhead compartment and took my seat. When the plane was nearly full and we were about to take off, I saw a Mexican lady, a very short, quite elderly lady, walking past me down the aisle with her luggage. She was struggling with her bag; the overheads were almost entirely full and she couldn't find anywhere to put it. I wasn't sure she was going to be able lift her bag to the locker in any case, and I was just getting out of my seat to give her a hand when another passenger, a man who looked like he was on a business trip, started to get frustrated. He said something to the lady, in English – something like, "Can you hurry up, please, because we're about to take off?" She just smiled vaguely and kept on looking for a place to put her luggage. She clearly didn't understand what he was saying. The man got more upset, and said the same thing again, only louder, and she looked a bit startled but didn't respond. He became even more irritated and raised his voice again.

The whole thing was turning into a bit of a scene. The old lady started to look alarmed. I stood up and said to the guy, in Spanish, *"No te entiende"* ('she doesn't understand you'). He turned around with an air of impatience and looked at me blankly. I said a little louder, still in Spanish, *"No te entiende."* He sat there staring at me, and I said in an even louder voice, *"No te entiende!"* The guy looked like he was going to get out of his seat and have a go at me, and I could see a flight attendant heading our way because of the raised voices. At that point I said to him, in English, in a lower voice, "That's exactly what's happening to her. She doesn't understand a word you're saying. The fact that you're saying it louder doesn't make it easier to understand. What you're doing is creating a tense emotional state that isn't helping anybody. Let me help the lady so we can all get going." He looked pretty mad at first, but then he backed off and said something like, "OK, buddy, whatever. Just don't want this flight to get held up," and settled back down in his seat. The flight attendant gave me a hand, we got the old lady's luggage into the overhead and the flight got on its way.

I tell that story to people at the retreat, and it helps them understand that it doesn't matter what you say to the horse, because it doesn't understand, and saying the same thing in a different tone of voice doesn't make any difference. Some people try to give the horse orders. They say *"Vamos!"* – Let's go! – in a commanding voice. Doesn't work. Some try to sweet talk the horse, patting it and stoking it or putting their arms around its neck and saying, "Horsey, horsey, I love you!" That doesn't work either. And then those people get irritated and decide this is a "stupid horse" that's just being difficult. But the horse just gets on with the business of being a horse and grazes on some grass and ignores the person or moves away. The one thing it definitely doesn't do is follow that person when they are trying to lead it somewhere, because it doesn't feel any emotional connection with them. If someone is anxious but pretending to be confident, the horse won't follow them either. Horses pick up on the subtle, nonverbal emotional and energetic signs that humans often miss.

After a few of these failed attempts, I ask people to stand by the horse, and start to tell a story, as if they were telling it to a friend, about some important thing in their life; something they feel deeply about. I suggest they close their eyes and try to forget where they are and what they're doing and just tell the story. When they get to the point in that story where they begin to feel emotional – maybe they start to feel a little tearful, if it's a sad story from their life, or they start to feel elated and joyful if it's a happy story – we ask them to start to move. Nearly every time, the horse will follow them. It will recognize the genuine emotion and there will be a connection between them. The horse wants to live, and its first reaction is one of caution and fear. If it feels safe, and you are merely stupid and annoying, it will happily ignore you. But if you establish an emotional connection so that the horse trusts you, it will follow you. If the horse doesn't trust you, it won't move. Or the horse will set off in some completely different direction, following its own horse agenda. And because the horse is much stronger than you, nothing you can do physically will make it change its mind. End of story.

It's a powerful lesson. It reminds leaders that words and logic are far less important than emotion. People (and horses) follow people they trust and feel a connection with, not those who say clever things that don't connect with them at an emotional level. When people in the group manage to make that connection with the horse and it begins to follow them, they are exhilarated. It is genuinely exciting to find that you can create a nonverbal emotional connection to a different species and form a kind of relationship. Horses seek leadership within a group, but they don't respond to force or hierarchy. They respond to leaders who project calmness, clarity and confidence – qualities that inspire trust and safety. Dominance and control don't work; collaboration and mutual respect do. This shift from 'power over' them to 'power with' them fosters a more inclusive and collaborative team culture.

By the end of the retreat, participants have a far deeper understanding of how emotions, feelings and sensations impact their leadership, not just on a personal level, but within their organizations.

They begin to recognize how their emotional energy affects those around them and learn to manage it in a way that inspires trust and collaboration. They learn not to simply control their emotions, but to master them, using emotions as a tool for growth and connection and applying this mastery in every aspect of their leadership and their lives.

When they walk into a tough conversation with a colleague or address their teams during a crisis, instead of being overwhelmed by the emotions of the moment, they know how to ground themselves. They learn to identify the sensations of stress, acknowledge the emotions driving their reactions and choose a response that aligns with their leadership vision. Participants often describe feeling lighter, more centered and more capable of handling emotional challenges. They gain practical tools to recognize when an emotion is taking control, shift into a more productive emotional state and lead with authenticity, using their emotions as a source of connection rather than a barrier.

This transformation doesn't just benefit them as individuals, it ripples outward, improving their leadership, relationships and organizational impact. Because horses are herd animals and their behavior naturally mirrors group dynamics, working with horses in this way can help explore how well teams are functioning and their collective emotional state. If a team approaches a horse with mixed energy, for example – some confident, some hesitant – the horse may become confused or resist engagement. This mirrors what happens in teams when there's a lack of alignment or clarity. Conversely, when the group is aligned in its energy and intentions, the horse responds with trust and cooperation, demonstrating the power of collective focus.

Teams often struggle with unresolved conflict or unmanaged emotions, which can lead to breakdowns in communication and productivity. Horses help participants practice emotional regulation in real-time. Someone who's feeling frustrated during an exercise might notice the horse resisting. The horse's reaction becomes a safe, non-judgemental way to explore and address the root of that frustration.

Team members learn how their emotions impact others and how to shift into states that encourage collaboration and problem-solving.

Horses teach participants to lead with inclusion.

These lessons translate directly to organizational dynamics, as leaders learn to invite participation rather than impose authority, and teams learn the value of listening and adapting to each other's needs. After the retreat, participants bring these lessons back to their organizations, leading to tangible improvements in team dynamics. Some examples include:

- **Improved Communication:** Teams become more open and transparent, addressing underlying issues before they escalate.

- **Stronger Trust:** Leaders build deeper trust with their teams by leading authentically and emotionally aligning with their vision.

- **Enhanced Problem-Solving:** Emotional awareness helps teams navigate conflicts and challenges with greater creativity and cooperation.

- **Increased Engagement:** Teams feel more connected and valued when leaders lead with emotional intelligence and authenticity.

Working with the horses helps demonstrate the essential need to connect our emotions with our words. Just as the horse has no interest in any of the words that may come out of our mouth until it senses that the words are said with real feeling, so our colleagues, friends and associates are looking for the emotional link between what we say and what they sense we are really feeling.

Our obsession with logic and reason sometimes causes us to forget this basic fact of life and believe that people can be genuinely moved by words and the force of argument. We have to engage with colleagues at a relatable, emotional, human level. Saying the same thing over and over again (even in a louder voice) will not have the right effect. And 'communicating' with someone while you're staring at your computer and saying, distractedly, "Yeah, great, just go do that, thanks," is not making any meaningful connection with them at all. The emotion is what makes the connection between the logic – the business plan that makes absolute sense – and the action. It provides the motivation everyone needs if they are going to change their behavior even one tiny little bit.

In business leadership, our emotions can have a direct effect on our ability to lead effectively and achieve the level of success we're capable of. Our emotions can help us, or they can hold us back. Let me give you an example.

I have a client named Santiago Martinez. He and I have worked together for many years. He is the director of a large group of businesses and the organization is very successful, largely because Santiago is an excellent leader. Delivering business success is not his problem. His problem is with his mindset, which is influenced by his emotional state.

Santiago is paid considerably less than he should be. If he were to apply for a CEO role in another organization, I am certain he would be offered the role; people would jump at the chance of having him run their business. I am also confident that he could increase his salary by at least 20% if he made the move. Maybe by 50%.

What's going on here?

The problem is something I've encountered several times in my career as a business coach. Santiago was hired by his company at a young age and has worked his way up the corporate ladder through hard work and talent. The company is a family business that has seen tremendous growth over the years, but it is still very much a family business and the family still see Santiago as the young kid they hired 30 years ago. He joined the company as a teenager and is now in his late 40s. Every time Santiago asks for a pay rise, the board, many of whom are family members, don't see him in the same light they would see an established candidate from an outside company. They still see young Santiago. And they say things like, "Oh, you need some money? Here's a $20,000 bonus. Just take it and you'll be fine. You deserve it!" They fix the problem by giving 'young Santi' some metaphorical chocolates to keep him happy. But his base salary stays well lower than it should be.

Santiago knows he is underpaid and undervalued, but he sees this only in the logical sense. He doesn't see himself as having the value that he actually represents to the company. He also feels a bit trapped, emotionally. He is very loyal to the family, because he has benefited from his success and from the company's growth. It's not as if Santiago hasn't grown financially, personally speaking. There is a part of him that feels, "The family have taken care of me. I have a good life. We have a nice house, the children go to private schools, we have several nice vacations every year. They have helped me come all this way, since I was a teenager getting his first job. I shouldn't complain."

In a recent coaching session, I tried to get to the heart of the problem, which is an emotional problem. I asked Santiago this: "When you look at yourself, what do you see? Do you see a 47-year-old senior executive, or do you still see yourself as a 17-year-old intern? Or maybe as the 27-year-old who's beginning to make a name for himself, and getting promoted to his first manager's role? How are you behaving? How do you think your bosses see you? Because they know you're capable. That's why you've been here for over 30 years, and have the salary you have, and the position you have. Not necessarily the one that you deserve, by the way, but the one that you have."

Because Santiago currently serves as a kind of co-director of the company. Three or four years ago, the family hired a retired CEO from another group, a man in his late 60s. His brief was to help Santiago develop and, ideally, in time, for Santiago to become the group's CEO. Their thinking could not have been more obvious. They had invented a role that hadn't previously existed and brought in someone very experienced from outside because they were thinking, "We love Santiago, and we'd love for him to be CEO of our group one day, but he's obviously not ready yet. He needs help. We'll bring in this experienced guy who will help him grow."

But, of course, the co-director wasn't helping Santiago grow. He was holding him back. Despite the best of intentions, the fact that Santiago wasn't being allowed to stand on his own two feet was stopping him from developing into a potential chief executive. To make things worse, he and the co-director didn't agree on the way forward for the organization. Whenever there was an issue between them, Santiago would tell me how his co-director was arguing for this or for that, and he wasn't able to do things the way he wanted. He was constantly fighting the system that had been created for him, but it was not a fight that was well fought. Instead of fighting the system, he should have been creating the system he needed to achieve what he wanted. Santiago had a clear vision for how the group could develop and grow, given the right investment, but his co-director was only interested in keeping things stable and safe and not rocking the boat. This worried Santiago, because he was convinced the business needed to keep moving forward and not rest on its laurels.

In my conversations with Santiago, I said, "Let's look at this again from the emotional standpoint. Why did the board make that decision? Why did they create this new role that is supposedly designed to help you grow and develop, but is in fact holding you back? It's because they still don't see you as a potential CEO. They would like you to get there, but when they look at you, they don't see a CEO. Not yet. They still see 'young Santi.' From the logical standpoint, you know you're capable of fulfilling this role. But you don't see yourself at that level. Emotionally, you don't have the guts to go and stand in front of the board and show them your plan, and demand what you know you deserve. Which is to be made CEO."

It was harsh of me to say that Santiago didn't have the guts, but it was true. He winced, but kept listening. We started to go through the steps of the meeting he needed to have with the board.

"You have the credentials and the experience," I told him. "If the board was going to hire an outside CEO, would you have all the same qualifications?"

Santiago thought for a bit and acknowledged that he did.

"If you went for a CEO role with another organization, would you get the job?

He looked a bit uncertain but acknowledged in the end that he probably would be offered the position.

"Of course you would. So if you go to the board and say you want to be made CEO, it would make logical sense for them to say 'Yes.' The question is, why they are saying 'No?' And the answer is because they are still seeing 'young Santi,' whom they like and admire, but they are not seeing 'Our CEO, Señor Martinez.'"

At Santiago's level in the organization, a significant aspect of the role becomes about managing the board. It's probably more about managing the board than it is about managing the company, because the people who report to you should be running the business, and most of your job should be about your vision for the company and the future. Santiago had not yet made that transition.

I asked him to show me his agenda for the next board meeting, but he had told me about past sessions, and they followed a clear pattern.

I said, "OK, let's put this agenda aside for the moment. What's the first thing the board is going to ask you? Because you go into a board meeting and you can have an agenda, but we both know the president or one of the board members is going to raise a question before everything starts, and that sets the tone of the meeting. What's the first thing they usually ask?"

I knew the answer, because he had told me several times.

"The first thing they ask is always about the wealth of the corporation," Santiago confirmed. "How is the net worth of the family growing? That's their first concern. Once they're happy about the organization's basic profitability, we can get round to discussing the rest of the agenda. But the bottom line is the bottom line!"

Santiago smiled briefly. It was nice to see him look happy. Normally in our sessions he looked a bit downtrodden and depressed.

We talked about how Santiago should focus on profitability from the outset. He should open the meeting by reassuring them that everything was on track, as it nearly always was, but then set the tone by raising the prospect of even better results in the future. He should tell them how he had a plan to drive the organization to even greater profitability. That way, he would definitely have their attention.

Santiago's real priority was to persuade the board he needed a new corporate structure, and that he needed to add some new positions to allow for further growth. But if he started the conversation with a list of all the new positions he wanted to create, the board's first reaction would be, "Whoa, hold on! Why do have to spend all this money? Why can't we manage with what we have?" The tactical approach would be to start with the desired end: to paint a picture of further growth and improved profitability – and, therefore, greater wealth – and to demonstrate that, to get from here to this improved position, there would need to be investment.

Now we had to get to the emotional part of the process.

"How are you going to behave when you go into this meeting?" I asked. "How are you going to be connecting with the board? What's the narrative? What are the key words you're going to use? How are you going to feel empowered? Also, which of the board members' support do you most need, and how are you going to get them to be your allies? Because every board member has their own personal agenda. It doesn't matter how small or big the business is, every board member has a personal agenda, whether it's about financial gain, or status, or recognition. There's always something everyone most wants. Your job is to understand what those are, because then you can change the emotions in your favor. Because we're negotiating. That's all we're doing. The goal that you want to achieve is higher staffing levels and a new corporate structure that will enable further growth. And that goal makes absolute sense – it's completely logical – because the board wants a better return on their investment. They want you to open new stores. They want you to maintain good relationships with key stakeholders. They want you to ensure you're in compliance with government regulations. They want to keep growing net profits. None of that is going to go away; there's going to be more and more work involved as the company continues to grow. So that's why you need a new structure, because you can't keep doing everything yourself and also achieve significant growth. You're telling me they're not willing to hire another seven people when they understand what that's going to do to their net worth? And then a huge part of that vision is that you must become CEO. How are you going to achieve this growth with one hand tied behind your back and a co-director who doesn't share your vision for growth?"

Santiago pulled a face that let me know exactly how he felt.

The next question was personal.

"So, Santiago, how are you going to present yourself? Are you still going to be the 27-year-old young man going to the board, frightened to demand that they authorize this plan of action? You're spelling out the possibility of further growth and, inevitably, there is some risk that comes with that. There is an investment to be made, and every investment carries risk. But, in your considered professional opinion, you will be able to deliver the forecast results of that investment. But only if they make you CEO. There's a prize to be had for them, but they have to make you CEO to get the prize. There's an element of threat in that, but it's necessary. Because they take you for granted. They still see 'young Santi.' He's great, but he's not the boss. Well, now Santiago must be the boss, calling the shots. If you want all this – higher growth and more wealth – then you have to put Santiago in charge."

I could see him thinking, but sensed he was still reluctant. I didn't think he could see himself laying it on the line like that.

I looked at him earnestly. "What's the worst that could happen?" I asked. "Seriously, what's the worst thing that could happen if you present that strategy to the board and demand to be made CEO?"

Santiago looked miserable. "Well, they're probably going to fire me. They're going to say I've gone crazy and I'm just spending their money and trying to sideline my co-director and I'm not ready to take over as CEO."

"But would they, really?" I asked. "After you helped the company grow by a factor of seven or eight times over the years? After nearly two decades of being the main person responsible for delivering profits, year after year? Do you really believe they're going to fire you?"

Santiago looked more thoughtful. He sat back in his chair

"Well, probably not."

"And anyway, what do you have to lose? What you have to *gain* is credibility. That you are the person they need to call the shots and the business needs to rest on your shoulders. Because once they see you as the person in charge and the person who is in control of taking the company to further growth and more profitability, the compensation is going to follow. That's not going to be hard. They've been seeing results year after year. They see you *managing* the business, but they don't see you *in charge* of the company. Big difference. They think, 'Sure, Santiago can manage the company, but can he be in charge? He probably needs this other person that we appointed, this co-director, to guide him.'"

I could sense some tectonic shifts happening in Santiago's mind. A look of real resolve came into his eye. I kept going.

"But, at some point, they are going to see you as being in charge. As being the only one. The only way that can happen is for you to show them. And once you show them and make those changes to drive more growth, compensation is going to follow."

A glint of battle had appeared in Santiago's eye, which was exactly what I wanted to see.

I tried to drive home my advantage.

"And the downside, for you, is ... nothing. It's all upside. So they fire you – which is not going to happen. I guarantee that in less than a week, you will have seven job offers, because you're well known in the industry. You have excellent relationships with all the major players.

If I call any of them and ask, 'Who is Santiago Martinez?' what do you think they're going to tell me? The biggest problem is you still can't believe that in your heart. You know it in your mind, but you don't believe it in your heart. What do we need to do for you to believe it, to have that boost of self-esteem that's going to catapult you into a different spectrum? All of a sudden, you're going to feel that you're not the manager anymore, you're the CEO. You just need to believe in yourself. You need to see yourself as CEO Martinez, not young Santi anymore."

Santiago thanked me and stood up decisively. We shook hands and said goodbye to each other. As I left the office, I could see that he had turned around and was staring pensively out the window. He looked a little taller somehow. As I said goodbye to Santiago's personal assistant on my way out, I couldn't stop myself from smiling.

"Good meeting?" she asked brightly.

"I think so," I said, still smiling. "Very good."

Although there was fault on both sides – with Santiago as well as with the family – I recognized his inability to fully inhabit his adult role. It's something I see a lot with my younger clients. I have been working with many of them for more than 20 years, and sometimes I had worked with their fathers before them. I remember a recent conversation I had with Santiago. His father had recently died. Santiago was only a few years away from being 50 years old, and I asked him how old he had been when his father was 50. He told me he had been about 15. I asked him to describe what his father had seemed like to him at that time. And the answer, of course, was that he had seen his father as his father – the head of the family, mature, well established, respected in his community. He was 'Mr. Martinez.' I asked him to think about why he didn't see himself like that at roughly the same age. Why he didn't see that he was now Mr. Martinez, and not young Santi anymore? He smiled, but I didn't think he really understood what I was driving at.

It's an issue I see a lot with this generation, because we want to remain young. We don't want to see ourselves as old, which also means we don't want to assume the responsibility that comes with age. It's a big issue. It's probably one of the biggest things that I work with in my coaching.

I was with a group recently, around half of whom were aged 50–55, and we were talking about this issue. I was saying, "Guys, I worked with your fathers when I was 30, and your fathers were 50-something. The way you guys are behaving in these meetings, it's like you're still 35. But you have the whole wealth of your families on your shoulders. And in business terms, it's not like you have $1million or $2 million on your shoulders. You guys have hundreds of millions on your shoulders."

It was interesting to me that quite a few of the group really stopped and reflected on that. Because it's OK to feel young. As we all stay fitter and healthier for longer, we effectively stay younger for longer. But we also need to accept that we have grown up and taken on adult responsibilities. We are *the grown ups in the room*, and we have to accept the responsibility that goes with that. Our employees, our sons and daughters and the whole younger generation, are looking to us for wisdom and maturity. We need to accept what we have become and fully inhabit our roles. Otherwise, as Santiago was in danger of doing, we can't realize our full potential.

This chapter on emotions transitions from the grounding force of logic to the dynamic, often untapped power of emotional intelligence in leadership and life. As I reflect on this, I'm reminded that, while logic structures our plans and tactics execute them, emotion is the connective tissue that binds them both. It is the spark that transforms a well-thought-out strategy into action, motivation and results.

HUMANS ARE EMOTIONAL BEINGS FIRST

The idea that people are first emotional and then rational isn't merely anecdotal. It's deeply rooted in psychology and neuroscience. Research by neuroscientist Antonio Damasio, a professor of Psychology, Philosophy and Neurology at the University of Southern California, has shown that emotions play a critical role in decision-making. Damasio's *Somatic Marker Hypothesis* posits that emotions are essential for making effective choices, as they provide a shortcut to help us weigh options and predict outcomes based on past experiences. He suggests that rationality, while invaluable, often arrives later, shaped by culture, education and life experience.

This explains why decisions that seem logical on the surface can still feel 'off' emotionally. For leaders like Santiago Martinez, failing to recognize and align their emotions with their logical goals created a disconnect. His logical capabilities were unquestionable, but it was his emotional state – his self-perception and limiting belief in his worth – that held him back from achieving the next level of leadership.

The lesson here is clear: we must recognize our emotional drivers and the emotions of those around us to truly move forward. Leaders must accept that people are not machines that respond purely to data or directives; they are emotional beings whose motivations are deeply personal.

THE ROLE OF EMOTIONAL INTELLIGENCE IN LEADERSHIP

In both the story of Santiago and the lessons from working with horses, we see the vital importance of emotional intelligence. Psychologist Daniel Goleman's framework of emotional intelligence – self-awareness, self-regulation, motivation, empathy and social skills – offers a useful lens to understand the power of emotions in leadership. Santiago's journey reflected a gap in self-awareness and self-regulation; he was trapped in an outdated self-image and unable to emotionally step into the role of CEO. It was only when he began to embrace his worth, acknowledge his emotional blocks and shift his self-perception that he could begin to act with authority and confidence.

Similarly, the example of working with horses reveals the universal need for trust and emotional connection. Horses respond to emotions, not words or commands, mirroring how people respond to genuine leaders. This underscores the importance of empathy and authenticity in leadership. If we want people to follow us, we must engage them emotionally, creating trust, connection and a shared vision.

VISION AND SELF-KNOWLEDGE: THE BEDROCK OF EMOTIONAL LEADERSHIP

Emotional leadership starts with vision. In the accounts of Santiago and his board and the experiences of leaders working with horses, we see the transformative power of a clear and compelling vision. However, vision alone is not enough; it must be deeply tied to self-knowledge. For Santiago, understanding his own value and reframing how he saw himself was the turning point. For the leaders working with horses, connecting to their own emotions through storytelling was the key to unlocking trust and connection.

A strong vision acts as a guiding light, while self-knowledge ensures that the leader has the emotional resilience and authenticity to bring others along on the journey. This alignment of vision and self-awareness creates a powerful foundation for change.

EMOTION AS THE ULTIMATE MOTIVATOR

People do not act on logic alone. They act on emotion, which is why motivation is deeply tied to our emotional states. This chapter's central story highlights the importance of understanding individual motivations, as with Santiago's struggle to feel worthy of the role he logically deserves.

Drawing on The Ten Principal Motivators That Drive Leaders, detailed earlier in the book, some key motivators serve as a roadmap for unlocking this emotional engagement:

1. **Recognition**
   The consistent thread in all these stories is the human need to be seen, valued and appreciated. Recognition is not just about achievements; it's about acknowledging effort, struggles and growth.

2. **Purpose**
   I cited earlier something said by Nietzsche: "He who has a why to live for can bear almost any how." When leaders align individual purpose with organizational goals, they tap into an inexhaustible well of motivation.

3. **Belonging**
   The example of the old woman on the airplane reflects our universal need for connection and understanding. Leadership is about creating environments where people feel they belong and are supported.

These motivators are the levers that leaders must pull to inspire action and build trust. Recognizing and nurturing these drivers within teams creates a culture where logic and emotion work in harmony, driving exceptional results.

BRINGING LOGIC AND EMOTION TOGETHER

In leadership retreats, the interplay of logic and emotion is brought to life through storytelling and experiential learning. The exercise with horses demonstrates a profound truth: logic alone cannot lead. To lead effectively, you must connect emotionally—both with yourself and others.

This insight extends to the way we manage ourselves. Santiago's story reminds us that emotions can either propel us forward or hold us back. Leadership is about mastering both our logical capabilities and our emotional states, ensuring that they align with our vision and values.

THE EMOTIONAL FRAMEWORK FOR LEADERSHIP

As I reflect on this chapter, I return to the powerful realization that leadership is as much an emotional journey as it is a logical process. Vision, self-knowledge and empathy are the cornerstones of effective leadership. They allow us to engage deeply with our teams, creating the trust and motivation needed to achieve our goals.

In business, as in life, emotion is the engine that powers our plans. It is the unseen force that turns ideas into action, plans into progress, and goals into reality. When leaders harness the power of emotion, they unlock the true potential of their teams and themselves. As we continue on this journey of Logic, Emotion and Tactics, let us remember that emotion is not a weakness to be overcome but a strength to be embraced. It is a bridge that connects our goals to the people who help us achieve them.

CHAPTER 13

TACTICS

We've talked about logic and emotion. Now it is time to talk about tactics. Tactics are like the glue that binds together the logic and the emotion. Tactics are what we must use to turn our logical plan into action by attaching the force and energy of our emotions to our understanding of the plan. Without this emotional commitment, even though we want to achieve something, and even knowing that we *should* achieve this thing, our heart is not in it. We need to use the right tactics to attach the engine of our emotions to the vehicle that logic has designed for us.

In life, as in business, we have many strategies. Maybe we plan to go to college and get our degree and then get a job and work our way up the ladder. Maybe we want start work straightaway, to begin making money and saving up for the things we want in life: a car, a house, a decent life for our families. Maybe we're clever at making videos on social media and plan to become a social influencer. We all have our strategies and our plans, but whether we achieve what we most want in life is no simple matter. It's not straightforward. There are many small decisions we have to make along the way. It's easy to make a misstep that sets us back. These small but essential decisions are our tactics in life.

To make things happen, there are three things we need above all else if our tactics are going to be successful. We need **discipline**; we need **agility**; we need **resilience**.

All the important things we want to achieve need discipline; we have to apply ourselves and keep working hard to reach our goals. We also need to be agile: we need to be able to adapt when circumstances change; to duck and weave and find new ways of achieving our objectives. And we need to be resilient. When we get knocked back, we have to be able to pick ourselves up, dust ourselves off, and start all over again.

It's the same in business: our organizations need to be disciplined, agile and resilient. But these things only happen through people. We can have the best strategies in the world – the best marketing strategy, the best financial strategy, the best sales strategy. But we need people to bring these strategies to life and make things actually happen. This is where a lot of businesses come unstuck. They fail because they don't align their business strategies with the personal lives of the people who implement them. Things only happen through people. If there is one lesson I'd like you to take from this book, it is the need to align our business goals with the personal goals of the people who are carrying out the plan.

The most important job of any manager is to break down the wider business strategy into smaller objectives that people can understand and relate to, and make sure they can see how achieving those will make their own lives better in some way. I'll give you an example from a startup business I was working with quite recently.

I had helped them develop their business strategy and their sales and marketing strategies. We had created the narratives they wanted salespeople to use with clients and put all the systems in place to help create a smooth customer journey. The financial strategy made sense and was capable of delivering the cash flow the company would need to operate successfully. On paper, it looked great. But after about six months, the founders called me back in. It wasn't working out for them. Their new company was struggling.

I worked with the team to look at the operational side of things. What I found was exactly the kind of situation a lot of young companies find themselves in. Nothing was running smoothly. Little things weren't getting done, and the little things snowballed into bigger and bigger things that were causing real problems. Everybody was spending all their time fighting fires and trying to fix things that weren't working properly, and nobody could find the time to look at the bigger picture and figure out the fundamental things that were going wrong. I talked to the team and found all the usual personal issues. There was John, who was coming out of a breakup with his girlfriend. There was Emily, who was having issues with her son. There were people who were in their first or second jobs who were very keen and eager, but they needed a lot of advice and guidance, and managers were struggling to find the time to help them. There was Miguel, whose father was dying, and who had a lot of family matters to sort out. In a nutshell, it was a collection of all the usual human issues that every team has.

I'm not saying that the company had hired the wrong people, because if they had fired everyone on the spot and hired an entirely new team, they would just have acquired a new set of human beings with similar issues in their lives. Everyone has personal issues of various kinds, and we are more emotionally connected to our personal lives than to a business strategy. That's entirely normal and part of life. Leaders need to know how to align their business plans and their business strategies with the personal lives of the people on their team. This may involve their compensation plan but will definitely involve aligning the things that need to be achieved for the business with what each person wants to achieve in their own life. All the people in this team were happy to be there. They wanted to work and make money, and they wanted the new business to succeed, but they were not as focused on the business's success as the business founders were. They had other things going on in their lives that demanded their attention.

Leaders need to create an environment that helps people achieve the **discipline** they need to get the essentials of the business done, and done consistently. It's no good if we operate brilliantly for one month, but then things begin to get ragged and fall apart. We need both a system and the ongoing motivation to keep operational discipline in place month after month. The team also needs to be **agile**, and able to respond to the inevitable glitches and problems that real life throws in the path of the best-laid plans. Finally, the team needs to be **resilient**, so that they stay motivated and are prepared to come into work, day after day, and find fixes for the various issues that keep coming their way.

The only way the team can achieve this is if they are constantly aware, literally minute by minute, of how the business's strategies and their own personal strategies align. They need to think something like this:

"If I can close this sale – or keep this customer happy or hit the target for the week – then we move toward that place we all talked about, which is a better place for me. The company continues to be successful, and we all keep our jobs."

Or, "If I can achieve this, then I get one step closer to that promotion that will mean our life at home gets a lot more comfortable."

Or, "I really believe in what we're trying to achieve here as an organization, and anything I can do to help us move forward is rewarding and satisfying for me."

A huge part of how leaders can achieve this is down to narrative and storytelling. I'm going to talk about this a lot more in the next chapter. Every organization needs to have a compelling and believable narrative. The real skill for leaders at every level is in finding a way to tell the story that relates our business journeys to our employees' personal journeys; to where they are now and where they want to get to.

If we want to relate people's personal journeys to the business's journey, how do we measure progress? How do we know how we're doing?

It's not complicated, but it's very important. If I want to get fitter, for example, I need some kind of measure as to how I'm progressing. Is it how far I can run? How fast I can run? Is it my body mass index? Is it that I am losing fat and putting on muscle? Whatever it is, I need something that tells me I am making progress toward my goal.

We talked about the Triumphometer earlier when we were thinking about Life Plans. This wonderful tool works just as well in a business context as it does in our personal lives.

To work the Triumphometer I need to know two things: Where are you today, and where do you want to be in three months and six months? Once we know that, we can define these stages and see what needs to be done to get you there. Let's start working on that. What skills and knowledge do you need to be able to do a great job and hit these targets – these KPIs? Do we understand what those performance measures are? These targets and measures will let me know I am moving in the right direction. Every minor success will ratchet my individual Triumphometer up to a higher level. And if the leader has done their job and aligned the business objectives with my personal goals – when I'm moving toward achieving the personal goals on my Triumphometer – the company is moving toward achieving its business goals also.

I'd like to show you a good example of the Triumphometer in action. The startup company we were just talking about was in the auto sector, like many of my clients. They were a car dealership, so the main problem was that they weren't selling enough cars. There were other problems too, as we saw: operational problems. Little things that kept going wrong that led to missed appointments, unhappy customers and late collection of payment because of various unresolved issues. All those things were adding up to enough of a headache to cause the company real problems. But the main problem was that they weren't selling enough vehicles.

We sat down and looked at the problem, and it soon became clear that the sales team were seeing enough clients, and delivering the sales narrative that had been agreed on, and doing demo drives and showing people the various finance options. They were lining up enough potential sales. The market was big enough and the marketing strategy was working – enough people were coming through the door and hearing the sales narrative – but too many of those potential sales were not getting finalized. They were disappearing. We had to imagine that most of the people who were seriously interested in buying a vehicle did go on to buy a vehicle, so most of those lost sales must have gone to one of the company's competitors.

The average time between a customer showing real interest in buying a car, taking a demo drive, getting a quote on the finances and everything else before making a final decision is two to three days. On average, if a customer is showing real interest, the deal can be closed and the contract signed within two to three days. But for this dealership, the average time for each salesperson was seven days. And the longer it took to close the deal and sign a contract, the more likely it was that the sale would be lost. Some 80–90% of deals should be closed within three days. As the number of days after the initial expression of interest goes up, so the likelihood that the sale will be closed goes down. Instead of the 80–90% being closed within a few days, the percentage goes down to 50%, 40% and 30% as days go by.

The salespeople would always have a reason why a deal hadn't gone through. "He said he wanted to talk to his wife, and he hasn't got back to me." "She was going on vacation and told me she would make her decision when she got back, so she'll probably pop in next week." "They wanted to go away and look at their finances before they sign." And so on and so forth. And because there were always new customers coming through the door, the salespeople would focus on the new potential sales and forget about the client they hadn't heard from for a week or more.

All sales operations work with what they call 'the funnel.' If you're selling cars, you start with a large number of people in the area who might have an interest in buying a vehicle, and then you narrow that down to the number who are in your immediate vicinity who might see your showroom or be exposed to your marketing materials, and then to the number who walk in the door, and then to the few who get seriously interested in a vehicle and ask for a demo drive. It's all very logical – you start with a fairly large number, which is the number of people who might conceivably buy a vehicle from you, and as they work their way down through the funnel, you end up with the number who actually end up buying. a vehicle.

The most interesting number is probably the percentage of customers who come into the showroom and express real interest in a vehicle and then go on to actually make a purchase – but not necessarily from your dealership. You had a good chance of making a sale, and you would expect to close a certain percentage of those sales. Let's say, for example, that you expect to close 15% of those sales. That means for every 20 customers who show a real interest in buying a vehicle, you make three sales. And maybe everyone is happy with that. But another way of seeing it is that you've failed to make a sale to the other 17 people who were legitimately interested in buying a vehicle from you but never did. Each sale was taking too long. Too many potential customers were falling by the wayside because the salespeople weren't finalizing the sales quickly enough and prospects were drifting away.

When we sat down and I looked at the sales funnel numbers with the founders of this company, they all had the same reaction. They were getting enough leads – enough potential sales to interested customers – and they all agreed they should be selling more cars.

I've talked a lot about the power of narrative. It's something I use all the time in my business. In this instance, I told the managers two different stories I knew they would be able to relate to, that would bring the issue to life for them and help them act on it.

"You've got your funnel, full of leads," I told them. "Customers who have expressed real interest in making a purchase. But underneath the funnel is a burner – like a fire; a barbecue. The leads are like the raw food that has to be cooked, and the food is coming out of the funnel and falling onto the burner. But if it stays on the burner too long, it's going to get burned and ruined. If you were running a restaurant kitchen, you couldn't sell the ruined food; you'd have to throw it away. That's what's happening to your leads. They're being left on the burner too long and they're getting burned – destroyed – because the deals aren't being closed quickly enough. For every sale that's left unclosed for more than three days, your chance of closing it falls away dramatically. You've got enough leads coming onto the burner to hit your targets, but you're leaving too many of them on the burner."

Nobody had a problem with that. They looked at the funnel and knew there was enough potential business coming through the door, so they could see that the problem lay with the burner.

"OK" I said. "Here's another story. I'm going to take you all to a football match. And it's an important match for your team."

Someone said, "Thank you very much!" and they all laughed.

I smiled. "OK – but, actually, I will! If we can turn this around together, I will take us to that match. That's a promise."

There was some smiling and joking and it was nice to see the mood lift a little. Everyone had been very anxious about the business not working out the way it should. I needed to see people's heads lifting.

I went on with the story.

"At the game, for the first half of the match, you're not allowed to watch the game on the pitch. You are only allowed to look at the scoreboard. Because the score is all that matters, right?"

More laughter.

"It's a serious point," I said. "Because that's what you're doing with your 15% conversion rate or whatever it is. You're focused on the percentage of sales the team are making from their leads, and you know it's not high enough but you're not thinking about the process that leads to that figure. You're focused on the output, not on the process – the scoreboard instead of the pitch."

I noticed a few people pulling faces and nodding their heads in a 'that's an interesting point' sort of way.

I kept going.

"Now, for the second half, you're allowed to actually watch the match. But when your team nearly scores a goal, you're not allowed to react in any way. We're only going to cheer if the team actually scores a goal. If a shot from our striker goes inches wide, or the opposing goalkeeper just tips it over the bar, we're not going to show any emotion. We're not going to throw up our arms in excitement but then clutch our heads and groan."

I mimed the actions and there was more laughter.

"And we're definitely not going shout and cheer and applaud the team to encourage them to try again. They didn't score, so that's that. We're not going to turn to each other and say, 'That was so close! Such a brilliant move! If we keep playing like this, we're definitely going to score soon.' We're not going to do any of that. We're not going to applaud and let the team know we can see that was a great move that could so easily have been a goal. We're going to just watch in stony silence. We only cheer and shout when we actually score a goal."

I could see that a few people were beginning to get the point.

"Because that's what we're doing with the funnel and the burner," I said. "Our team is getting really close to scoring a goal – making a sale – and we're ignoring them. We're not encouraging them and cheering them on and thinking about what we have to do to turn that exciting lead into a sale.

"We're not making that connection. We're just waiting for the result. The moment that we start looking at the process and we start enjoying the process, really enjoying it, enjoying every step, you're going to see your team getting more engaged. And the moment you see the team getting more engaged, you're going to start winning more games – selling more vehicles."

I started to get to my conclusion.

"Right now, you're making a logical plan, but you're not following on with the emotion. You're not using the tactics that will connect the logic to the emotion. You're holding meetings, and you're just listening to the report. 'We closed 15% of the deals. We've got to try harder.' Where's the heart? Where's the emotion? Where are the cheerleaders and the marching band? Where's the encouragement that's going to keep your people engaged eight hours a day trying to get the next sale?"

I suggested a tactical solution: let the salespeople do what they were good at – filling up the funnel – and make one of the management team responsible for looking after the 'burners.' That manager would be bonused on raising the number of leads that got converted into sales and he or she was going to get personally involved in helping the sales team raise the success rate.

At the start of the week, that manager could say, "We've got 20 sales on the burner. You three guys, you haven't got anything on the burner so your job is clear: let's get some leads lined up and onto the fire. Now, what's the state of play with these 20 leads already on the burner?" The manager would supply the cheerleading and the excitement and the encouragement and remind the sales team of what would happen to their bonus if we could finalize a few more of the leads that were drifting away.

"Let's find out what's holding the sale up. Is there something we can do to close the deal? Are we losing the sale to a competitor? Is it about price? Is there anything else we can do to sweeten the deal and close the sale?"

People would start to become excited and involved instead of letting the old lead go and moving on to the next potential sale.

This is where the Triumphometer comes back into play. There are sales out there just waiting to be closed. Sales that have come a long way down the funnel, stalled at the final stage and stuck on the burner. Maybe there's an insurmountable problem – maybe the client has decided to buy from a different dealer, or not to buy at all right now. But maybe the sale can still be saved. Maybe the client needs just one more nudge, or one small concession, and the deal will go through.

For a salesperson, the Triumphometer needs to reflect two things: *Where are you today, in your own life, and where do you want to be in three months and six months?* It needs to be *personal*, otherwise the salesperson will not be emotionally engaged.

Let's think about one of the sales team, someone named Fred. Fred wants to buy a used SUV, using his staff discount. He needs to raise around $15,000 to make the purchase.

Let's go through the financial framework of the Triumphometer one more time.

1. DEFINE YOUR GOALS

› Start by identifying your desires and dreams. Fred's desire is to buy a used SUV like the ones he sees every day there at the dealership.

2. BREAK DOWN THE COSTS

› Next, break each goal into manageable financial increments. For example, if Fred needs to save $15,000 and he earns $300 in commission per client, that equates to 50 clients. If he wants to maintain his current lifestyle while saving an additional $15,000, he ideally needs to make 50 more sales over his usual tally. He thinks he can make an extra sale per week if he tries really hard, so his goal will take him a year to achieve. But it'll be worth it.

3. CREATE A DEDICATED SAVINGS ACCOUNTS

› Open a separate savings account for this target. As Fred makes an additional sale, every $300 goes into this dedicated account.

4. SET INCREMENTAL TARGETS

› Divide your efforts into manageable pieces. In Fred's case, if he can make his additional sale per week – not easy, but achievable – he makes $300 more each week: $300 x 52 = $15,600. Success!

If Fred's sales manager works with him to create this Triumphometer, monitoring progress toward his goal of buying the SUV, Fred will be constantly motivated to convert those leads sitting on the burner into sales. Fred gets his dream car, and the business begins to cut back on the sales being wasted because they're left too long on the burner. The Triumphometer has helped show Fred that he really can make that extra money to achieve his dream. And now that he has bought his SUV, he'll also now have an additional $1,200 per month over his normal income if he maintains the new, higher number of sales he's proved himself capable of achieving. Now is the time to revisit his Life Plan and his expenditure silos and see where that extra money will go. His lifestyle has begun to change, because what really matters is not how much money you make but the life you want to live.

By using tactics in this way, we are looking at the sales process, segmenting it and putting a focus on different parts of it. We're mapping the money-making journey we need to take and thinking about where things are going wrong and what solutions we can apply to make things work better. We're revisiting the definitions of people's roles and redefining them, so everyone knows what they're doing, and they're doing the thing that's adding the most value. We're relating the goals of the business to the personal dreams and desires of the team. We're choosing different KPIs and changing our dashboard. We're applying our business logic using the most effective tactics. We have our logic and our tactics – we're ready to go!

But the final question is always about emotion. The biggest question is always: *why* are we going to do it? Why is the manager going to do it? Why is the salesperson going to do it? Why are you, the director, going to do it? Why do you, the owner, want to do this? What is our role here as human beings? AI will soon be able to supply a lot of our business logic, and if I give all these plans to an AI bot and ask it to work out the best tactics to achieve our goals, it's going to create a set of tactics. But are they the best tactics for the actual human beings we have working for us right now? Are the tactics really going to resonate with John and Emily and Miguel at this precise part of their life plan? Only humans can supply the emotional connection – the cheerleading; the contagious emotional state that makes people understand the 'why,' and the emotional connection that means things actually get done.

Tactics are the glue that binds together our logical plans and the emotions that will motivate people to actually carry out the plans.

One final thought about something very important we cannot ignore when we think about tactics: the **enemies of tactics**.

One enemy of successful tactics is **perfectionism**. We try to do everything so perfectly that we never get to do it at all. We're always holding back because our plan is not good enough. It's not *perfect*.

Good enough beats perfect every time. Perfectionism is an enemy, not an ally.

Another enemy is **fear**. Fear of failure. "I don't want to try this because I'm setting myself up to fail. I'm signing up for something I think I can't deliver, and everyone will see me as a failure."

This is incredibly common, in every aspect of life. "I'm not going to commit to this and put my head over the parapet because then everyone will see that I'm going for it, and if I fail, they will know all about it and judge me." So we don't even try.

Finally, there is **self-doubt**. It's a lot like fear, but not quite the same. Fear is about being judged by others, but with self-doubt we are judging ourselves. "I'm not up to this. I'm just not good enough. I can't deliver the result everyone expects." We know we should do something, and we want to do it, but we are resisting ourselves. Our self-doubt is actively fighting our wish to make things happen.

You probably know people who are full of plans that never seem to come to fruition. They have wonderful dreams, but they can't make them come true, because they're obsessed with perfection, or full of fear and self-doubt. Some people get angry with themselves for failing, and that makes everything worse. They've failed to achieve their goal, and they're also bitter and angry about failing.

All of these **enemies of tactics** get in the way of **discipline**, **agility** and **resilience**. We have a plan, and we believe in the plan, but we find ourselves unable to take the first step down that road. We can't get started. We don't have the tactics that will let us link our understanding of the logic of the plan with our emotional commitment to making it happen. The enemies of tactics have gotten in the way.

The solution lies in better **narratives**. We are all the heroes of our own story. We set off on the adventure of our lives. We face many obstacles, which we strive to overcome using our special skills and ingenuity and with the help of long-standing friends and allies. People we meet on our journey, who either help us or thwart and betray us. In the end, we either triumph or we fail. If we fail, our story has become a tragedy – hopefully a glorious tragedy, where we at least tried, against all odds. But, if we prevail, we become true heroes.

Understanding our own narrative and helping to create good narratives for our colleagues and the people around us, is essential to the successful deployment of tactics. In the next chapter, we'll look more closely at the effective use of narrative and storytelling in business and in our personal lives.

The bridge between logic and emotion is action, and tactics are the steps that turn ideas into measurable outcomes. In life, as in business, tactics form the foundation of progress. They remind us that dreams without action remain fantasies. Success, whether it's personal growth, closing a sales deal or running a business, begins with disciplined, deliberate steps.

As I reflect on the stories in this chapter, the narrative of the **Triumphometer** stands out as a perfect metaphor. The Triumphometer helps us measure incremental progress by focusing not on the ultimate goal but on the daily actions that move us closer to it. It's not about achieving perfection but about starting – about recognizing that success is built on small, consistent victories.

STRATEGIC PLANNING AND EFFECTIVE COMMUNICATION

Strategic planning is the backbone of any logical process, but tactics make that plan operational. As illustrated with the car dealership story, knowing the conversion rates, the sales funnel and the timelines for closing deals were logical observations. But what turned this logic into results was **effective communication** – sharing the narrative of the funnel and the burner, engaging the team with stories that humanized the process, and encouraging them to reframe how they approached each lead. Stories became tools of alignment, and alignment became the driver of success.

This speaks to the critical role of storytelling in communication. When leaders share relatable narratives, they transform abstract goals into tangible actions. The moment we stop viewing results as cold numbers and start linking them to the personal aspirations of our teams, we create a culture where people feel empowered, emotionally engaged and motivated to perform.

AGILITY AND ADAPTABILITY

In the car dealership, the team had to learn agility – not by rewriting their strategies, but by adjusting their tactics to close sales faster. They shifted their focus from the endgame to the immediate steps that mattered. The agility described here mirrors the principles from the book *Doing Agile Right*, by the business consultants Darrell Rigby, Sarah Elk and Steve Berez. They suggest **small, iterative steps** with a focus on feedback loops. The burner metaphor introduced urgency, but the manager assigned to oversee the funnel brought adaptability, helping the team respond quickly to challenges and seize opportunities.

Similarly, the startup story highlights the importance of adapting tactics to the human realities of life. Whether it was Miguel dealing with family issues or Emily struggling with her son, understanding and aligning business objectives with personal circumstances allowed the company to regain momentum. Agility wasn't just about processes; it was about people.

DISCIPLINE: THE GLUE OF TACTICS

Discipline is the foundation of all tactical success. Whether it's making calls, scheduling meetings or following up on leads, discipline ensures consistency. The story of the delayed car sales exemplifies how a lack of discipline in closing leads can unravel a strategy. The Triumphometer helped instill discipline by breaking down the sales process into actionable steps. Each small triumph reinforced motivation and drove the team forward.

OVERCOMING THE ENEMIES OF TACTICS

The enemies of tactics – perfectionism, fear and self-doubt – are universal barriers. They stop us from taking the first step, creating a mental paralysis that disconnects us from the actions that could lead to progress. This chapter reminds us that action doesn't need to be perfect; it simply needs to start. The phrase '**good enough beats perfect every time**' is a powerful reminder that progress begins with imperfection.

These enemies are not just obstacles to individual actions; they also undermine team dynamics. By addressing these challenges openly and reframing narratives, leaders can build a culture of resilience and courage. The manager who took responsibility for the burner in the car dealership didn't demand perfection; he sought progress. This created an environment where taking risks and learning from failure became part of the process.

THE ROLE OF ADAPTIVE LEADERSHIP

As with everything we're discussing in this book, the principles of **adaptive leadership** resonate deeply here. Successful tactics depend on leaders who can diagnose challenges, align actions with both logic and emotion, and adjust quickly to shifting circumstances. An adaptive leader encourages experimentation and learning, fostering resilience in teams and individuals. It's about creating a sense of ownership and connection between personal goals and organizational objectives.

THE 10 MOTIVATORS IN ACTION

Tactics are most effective when aligned with human motivators. In this chapter's stories, these 10 motivators drive action:

1. RECOGNITION

Recognizing even small wins, like closing a lead quickly, reinforces discipline and builds confidence.

2. COMPETENCE

Encouraging team members to master each step of the process fosters pride and performance.

3. FREEDOM OF EXPRESSION

Open communication allowed salespeople to share barriers, enabling better tactical adjustments.

4. GROWTH

The Triumphometer was a tool for personal and professional growth, showing clear pathways to progress.

5. HAPPINESS

Addressing personal struggles like Miguel's family issues created a supportive environment, boosting morale.

6. FINANCIAL REWARDS

Linking success to commission incentivized disciplined action in the dealership's sales funnel.

7. PURPOSE AND MEANING

Framing tactics as a way to contribute to personal and organizational success gave team members a sense of mission.

8. AUTONOMY AND CONTROL

Empowering the 'burner manager' with clear responsibilities showcased trust and created accountability.

9. BELONGING AND CONNECTION

Collaborative problem-solving fostered a sense of teamwork and connection.

10. CHALLENGE AND MASTERY

Turning tactical actions into measurable goals created a sense of accomplishment and encouraged striving for mastery.

Tactics turn dreams into reality, ideas into actions and vision into measurable results. They require leaders to bridge logic and emotion, to create systems like the Triumphometer that track progress, and to motivate their teams through clear narratives and adaptive strategies.

Discipline, agility and resilience are the bedrock of successful tactics, but the real magic lies in the emotional connections leaders forge – connections that transform ordinary steps into extraordinary outcomes.

CHAPTER 14

NARRATIVE, STORYTELLING AND L.E.T.

Storytelling is one of the most powerful tools we have to combine the logical, emotional and tactical aspects of any situation. Every story has its own internal logic. It makes sense. But stories are also deeply emotional: they draw us into the world of the protagonists, whose struggles, triumphs and disasters we experience as if they were our own. Finally, stories have a very tactical dimension: they give us ideas about how to behave in various situations; provide us with role models; inspire us to take action.

Businesses often overlook or forget the power of storytelling. There are many examples of businesses that use great stories in their advertising (because the best ad agencies understand the huge power of storytelling) but never think to use this as a way of communicating internally, with their own colleagues and teams. I've seen several instances where the advertising guys get the essence of the organization's story so exactly right that the commercials – designed to appeal to consumers – are used internally as a kind of stand-in for organizational storytelling. Bosses play the commercial and say, "There you go, that's who we are." And, because the ads work at a logical, emotional and tactical level, people in the organization are convinced, moved and inspired. They look at the advertising and they think, "Yes, that is who we are. That's why I'm proud to work here."

A good example might be Avis, the car rental company. They acknowledged outright that they were in second place to Herz in their market, which was a radical approach when most advertising was about proclaiming market-leading strengths – being the biggest, the best. Avis made a strength of the fact that they had to try harder to win customers, and that they couldn't afford to be complacent or sloppy. The famous 'We Try Harder' campaign, written in 1962 by copywriter Paula Green for the ad agency Doyle Dane Bernbach, ran for 50 years, until it was finally replaced in 2012 by 'It's Your Space.' For more than half a century, the simple phrase 'We Try Harder' conjured up the essence of the Avis story. In three words, it told consumers that Avis cared about their customers and would go out of its way to make them happy. And it told everybody who worked there a story about who they were and how they should behave. "We do everything we can to give our customers a great experience. We may not be the biggest, but we think we're the best!"

I'm not saying that using the company's consumer advertising to inspire colleagues and encapsulate the story of the company is a bad idea. Far from it. But good storytelling is not the sole province of the marketing department and the advertising guys. Leaders can use the power of storytelling on a daily basis to set out their vision and engage the team. It takes a bit of practice to do it well, but anyone can do it. A powerful story tells itself. You don't have to be a great orator or a great actor to make an impact. Just tell a good story and let it work its magic.

There is another important aspect to storytelling. It's not only something we can use to explain our vision and our ideas to other people and inspire them in business, stories are hugely important in our personal lives. When we fully understand the story of our own lives, that helps us to play our role properly and feel fulfilled. Many people struggle in life because they haven't become the hero of their own story. They feel as if they have a walk-on part in someone else's story, because they haven't been able to tell themselves the story of their own lives in a way that helps them inhabit their role successfully – something we saw earlier in the story of Santiago. We'll hear more about what happened to Santiago's quest to become CEO at the end of this chapter.

The key elements of every good story were laid out in the mid-20th century by Joseph Campbell, an American professor of English literature who also worked in comparative mythology. Campbell looked at stories told from the dawn of recorded time to the present and found common themes.

Every story has a hero or heroine we can identify with. We first encounter them in their day-to-day life, going about their normal business, which helps to set the scene and provide the context for what follows. Then, something extraordinary happens that disrupts that everyday life and causes them to embark on an adventure. The hero likely has many doubts and reservations and resists this call to set off into the unknown, but in the end, they cross the threshold. They set off on their adventure, passing a point of no return. On their journey they meet people who help or hinder them: friends, allies and enemies. They face many challenges and tests and overcome these, sometimes through their own ingenuity and bravery, and sometimes with the help of others. Eventually, they come to the central ordeal: the obstacle they must overcome or fail in their quest. If they are successful, they get their reward and return home triumphant, bringing gifts and newfound wisdom.

Does that sound familiar? Do you find yourself thinking about how your own life could be fitted into that structure of unexpected challenges; setbacks and successes; obstacles faced and overcome? That's because, although several thousand years of human storytelling have built that structure into our folklore, it also mirrors how we all experience our lives. It's why we can all harness the power of storytelling so effectively.

Before we look a bit more at the power of storytelling, I'd like to tell you a story from my own experience.

One of my longest-standing clients, for more than 20 years, is named Michael. He's around 50 years old now, so I first met him when he was about 30. He had just taken over the business from his father, who cast a long shadow. A big, big shadow.

When we first met, the father's shadow was not a major issue. Michael was a dutiful son, and the relationship worked well enough, but only because Michael was quite submissive. He looked up to his father and his father was happy with that. The father was not so happy with the idea that Michael had to become his own man and that he would, one day, take over the business. That was what the father wanted, in theory: to pass on the business to his son. In practice, the father was finding that very difficult.

Michael was always extremely talented: bright and personable, with good business sense. He went through many things in his life: divorce, remarriage, kids. He matured, and the time came when he realized he needed to start leading his father. The moment had arrived when he should stop following his father, and it was up to him to take charge of the business. But, as you can imagine, the father was not happy about giving up the lead to his son.

Like many business founders, Michael's father had a big ego.

"This business only exists because of everything I did and all the things I have been through. I'm not going to let you destroy it!"

Michael had grown up surrounded by the stories about how the business was started.

"This room we are sitting in – this building – there was nothing here," the father would say. "I built all this!" All these stories, which were the foundational stories of the father's business, were like a rock that Michael was always carrying with him. A burden.

I worked with Michael to create a new narrative about his own vision for the company, and where it should be headed, and why it was different from the father's old vision. When you have a story that has been told to you since you were a child, which is the wonderful story of how your father built the company and created the wealth that sustains the family, it's a powerful thing. It's a living story – something the whole family lives with every day. So now we have to create another, more powerful story that can take over from the one Michael and his family have been hearing all their lives. We need to find a way to create another story that is a sequel to the first. The origin story is a great, powerful story, but things have moved on. There are new stories that need telling. That was book one, now we have to create book two, which begins where book one ends.

Michael needs to be able to tell this new story to the family and the board of directors and all his colleagues. Everyone will still honor the old story and tell it to remind themselves where they have come from, but now Michael has to undertake a new adventure of his own. He must overcome new obstacles and dangers before the company can arrive safely at its new destination. Michael also has to tell the story to his father who, of course, is going to resist it at first, because it reminds him that his own story is coming to an end. But, because he is a good father who loves his son and wants to see the business he has built continue to thrive, he will come to welcome the new story and hearing about the new adventures that lie ahead.

It's never easy, but it can always be achieved. When I coach businesses for family succession, this new, next-generation narrative is one of the biggest things we have to work on.

There was one extreme case I came across with a different client. The founder of the business, Emiliano, was reluctant to stop running the company, even when he had reached the age of 75 and should have been beginning a well-earned retirement. But when the family approached him about his successor, which was not an issue he ever talked about himself, Emiliano reacted as if the family were trying to kill him.

"You think I'm old and I can't think anymore, and you're trying to get rid of me!"

He became very bitter and announced that there would not be any succession.

"The day I die, you guys can decide who comes next. But I'm not dying any time in the next 25 years."

By which time he would have been 100 years old, of course. But that didn't seem impossible, because Emiliano was tough and strong and very stubborn!

Emiliano had two children: a daughter and a son. The son was the younger of the two, but he believed he should be the successor because he was a man. They were both involved in the business, but they couldn't agree on who should take over as President and CEO. As a result, they didn't have a unified story to present that had the power to overshadow the old story.

Intriguingly, it looks as if the job of doing that will fall to the next generation. Emiliano's two children are in their fifties now, and the daughter's own daughter, a woman in her twenties named Gabriela, is working at the company. I have been coaching her, as well as the son, and it seems to me that it is Gabriela who most has the grandfather's ear and is best able to tell a new story that he and everyone else can believe in. With so much family politics involved, it will not be easy, but my money is on Gabriela. I look forward to seeing how book one ends and to enjoying reading book two!

We talk a lot about the importance of a leader's vision, and for good reason. If an organization doesn't have a vision of where it is headed, it's directionless. It simply doesn't know where it's going or what its purpose is. People can't feel inspired and motivated if they don't feel that the work they do every day has any purpose or meaning.

The purpose can be very simple and straightforward – giving people something that brings them pleasure or makes their life a little better or easier in any way is deeply meaningful. But the only way to set out a vision and explain the purpose of what we do is to tell a story. There's no other way. The question then becomes, how well are we telling our story?

The good news is that every business venture has its own built-in, fascinating and true story. Every business starts with an idea and with a passion. Very few people (nobody that I know) starts a business just to make money. There are senior jobs that will deliver higher rewards than any small- to medium-sized business owner is likely to make in their lifetime, without all the stresses, strain and risk that goes with running your own business instead of being comfortably employed and seeing your paycheck turn up every month.

Some people might be happy running a business of any sort, in any sector, because they just want to be their own boss, but most business owners I know genuinely love the business area they operate in. They love selling cars, or clothes, or garden machinery, or they love running a restaurant or a gym or a florist. That means there's a fascinating story to be told about their dream, their passion, and their struggle to bring that business to life, nurture it along and make their dream come true.

Then there is the continuing story of how that business will change and grow and develop – what they want it to achieve and how they plan to get there. That has a lot of power. It's a story in itself, with a hero, an adventure and many obstacles that need to be overcome. People who work for the company will be excited to hear that story and to be a part of this new adventure. Where are we all headed? What's going to happen to us? What will it feel like when we achieve the vision? What will we tell our family and friends; what will we be saying to each other? Once we can describe the emotions we will have when we achieve the vision, we can create the story and it will be completely authentic. It won't be something out of a work of fiction – it has been created out of you. The story describes you as a leader and sets out your vision.

Now, it has to become your constant narrative.

There are two parts to any business story: the foundation story and the vision for the future. The foundation story needs to be told often: to everyone who joins the company; at major events; to folks chatting around the watercooler. Everyone should know the story well enough to be able to tell it to each other and to their friends and family. It should be like the story of Bill Hewlett and Dave Packard, founders of Hewlett Packard (now HP), who started their business in 1938. It was just the two of them making electronic equipment in the garage of Packard's house in Palo Alto, California, in what became known as Silicon Valley. Everybody who has ever worked for HP knows that story. It's so famous, and so influential, that many tech startups have tried to say they started off working out of a garage, even when it wasn't true.

The story was so powerful and had such staying power because it reflected the founders' determination to keep running their rapidly expanding business with an agile, small-company ethos. They sought alignment on core objectives, but gave employees latitude to get the job done in whatever they felt was the most effective way, rather than taking all their instructions from Hewlett and Packard themselves. The company kept its 'garage mentality' for a long time. The company has been through major corporate changes and seismic market shifts and Hewlett and Packard are now long dead, but I would bet money that everyone at HP still thinks about Bill and Dave in the garage of Dave's house, making audio oscillators to test sound equipment and making their first sale to Walt Disney Productions, a young studio that had just struck unexpected gold with the world's first full-length animated film, 1937's *Snow White and the Seven Dwarfs* – because Bill and Dave's story is a great story.

Let's go back to the basic principles of great storytelling. Bill and Dave in their garage was just the first act; the scene-setting. Next comes the many obstacles and challenges our heroes must overcome with the help of their colleagues, friends, family and others they encounter on their journey. Every business story has many such characters – people who work in manufacturing, sales, finance, marketing, maintenance and security. There are many external stakeholders and, of course, there are threats and obstacles in the form of competitors and market forces.

Weave them all into your story. Remind the team of the essential part they have to play in this adventure. The story needs to be told all the time if people are to stay focused and motivated; you can't simply tell it once and hope it will stick with people forever; it needs to be repeated over and over again. And when we are talking to different people, the story needs to be told slightly differently to reflect their role and their perspective. Martin, who is head of finance, needs to be told a slightly different story than Marianne, who has just joined as a sales trainee. And a good leader will know that one colleague has more buy-in if the story is linked to dancing in some way, whereas another is a big fan of Formula 1 racing who will relate to the story better in those terms. The emotional meaning the story has for them will be slightly different, even though its overarching narrative remains the same. We need to connect all the characters together and weave them into the storyline so we all share the same vision and we all want to reach our destination, regardless of our specific roles.

I often suggest that my clients go to a performance of a symphony orchestra and pay particular attention to the conductor. The conductor has their own specific vision of how the music should be played. The same composition conducted by two different maestros will have a very different emotional tone and impact. The conductor uses the various sections of the orchestra – the strings, woodwinds, brass, percussion, choir, a featured soloist – to create a performance that reflects their personal vision for what the music should convey to an audience. The conductor sets the tempo, volume and tone, leading the musicians via their own body language to convey the emotions they feel the music should express.

This is the job of any leader: to interact with the team through the days, months and years, so they can feel the leader's tempo, volume and emotion. The importance of simple body language is often overlooked. Leaders convey a great deal of information to their teams simply through the way they look: are they upbeat, optimistic and energetic, or anxious, distracted and downcast? But the most significant communication in business will always be verbal, and the most powerful verbal communication tool is the story.

The story will need to change and adapt as the company moves forward. The leader's vision must be unchanging – if the vision changes, people quickly become confused. And the story that explains the vision will need to be repeated on many occasions, until it is absorbed into the very fabric of the organization. But *goals* can change frequently to reflect changing circumstances:

if the data shows that we need to make an adjustment and plot a new course; when we sense that we are taking the wrong path and need to change short-term objectives, goals and the route that will lead to achieving our vision. If we've been pursuing one course of action for some time and it's not working, it may be that we need to change and adapt the narrative to explain how we will move forward differently. But the vision does not change.

As noted at the beginning of this chapter, stories are not only important in the world of business. We need powerful stories in our personal lives. We already have immensely powerful stories that we tell ourselves about our lives, but we often fail to make them explicit to ourselves. These stories can sometimes be very damaging. Many people tell a story about themselves in which they are not very successful. Deep down, they don't see themselves as clever, or talented, or likable or lovable. Whatever happened to them when they were younger to give them this internal story about themselves has become entrenched as the story of their lives. If they have any success, they start to suffer from imposter syndrome – feeling inadequate, and afraid of being exposed as a fraud – because of their inner story of failure.

We all suffer from moments of self-doubt. Almost everybody feels a touch of imposter syndrome from time to time. Anybody who doesn't probably has too high an opinion of themself. But for the people we're talking about, a story of inadequacy and failure has become the dominant story of their lives. They've stopped believing in their vision for a better future for themselves: they don't feel they deserve the level of success they have; they don't believe that it will last, and they fear they'll be revealed as the fake they feel themselves to be. They fail to do things they are perfectly capable of and then fall back on excuses for why things aren't going the way they should, effectively sabotaging their own efforts.

These personal stories need to be rewritten. We need a new story about ourselves. We need to start believing in ourselves again and telling a positive story to ourselves about our own lives. At certain levels of personal damage, this will only be possible through therapy with a skilled practitioner, but most of us are capable of doing it for ourselves after a period of deep reflection and with a real resolve to change. Take the time to think about how you would tell the story of your own life and then reframe it to accentuate the good things – the triumphs over adversity; the things you have accomplished that reveal your many wonderful qualities. See yourself as a success story. Celebrate your achievements and the things you are good at. The very act of putting a more positive spin on your life story will begin to make you feel better about yourself.

Let's go back to the story of Santiago, the executive who, despite all his success, was struggling to reposition himself in the eyes of the board, who still saw him as the 'young Santi' they had first employed decades earlier.

If you were to talk to anyone Santiago works with or to any of his clients – senior executives of major corporations – they would be amazed to hear this. Santiago is a recognized expert in the business; he knows his stuff. He's a great boss, and he's charming and fun to be around. Anyone who knows him would say without hesitation that he doesn't have a problem with self-esteem ... but, deep down, he does. When he talks to his superiors, the owners of the company, his head goes down. He accepts whatever they say and fails to persuade them to do what he feels should be done to take things forward, even when he's clearly right and they're wrong. Then he starts to make excuses to himself about his behavior. "Well, this happened because of these circumstances. There wasn't anything else I could do!" Later, he reviews these things and starts being creative and optimistic again, having great new ideas.

But when these get blocked, he goes back to his usual reaction and gets angry with himself and upset.

I had asked Santiago to create a vision for himself, and for the role he should have in the company. It wasn't about setting goals; what was lacking was the vision of who he should be and how others could see him. He had created a successful vision for the company; that wasn't a problem. What he was currently lacking was his own vision, a vision of his future self. He needed to tell himself a story in which he was *deservedly* chief executive of the company he had done so much to build into the success it had become. Once he understood that story and believed in it, the owners would believe it also, recognizing that he had crossed a threshold and was ready for the role of CEO.

The problems we face in life are never insurmountable. If we have faith in ourselves, we will be able to overcome them. Very often, the story we tell ourselves about who we are, what we're capable of and how other people see us is all that is holding us back.

I had suggested to Santiago that it was time for him to deliver an ultimatum to the board of the family business to which he felt so loyal. In particular, he had to convey this message to the head of the family himself, a man named Jorge. I told Santiago he had nothing to lose – he would be able to walk into a new role as CEO of any one of half a dozen other companies if his bold gambit failed – and he had everything to gain, because logic was telling us that he was right; he was the person best-placed to be CEO of the company.

Let's see how things played out.

As he walked into the boardroom, Santiago took a deep breath. He greeted everyone, family members and external board members, who were all more like old friends than simply colleagues. His co-director, Jonathan, was there, and Santiago greeted him briefly but avoided conversation.

Everyone took their seats around the boardroom table. As we've noted, it was customary for Santiago to make an initial report on the key numbers and any significant issues the company had faced since the last meeting or would likely face in the immediate future. It was also customary for someone – usually the head of the family – to immediately interrupt Santiago and ask that he cut straight to the chase and report on the company's financial position. Today was no different, but Santiago refused to be drawn.

"I'll come to that in due course, if I may. As you will see from your agenda, I have something important I would like to present to the board today which takes precedence. It has a direct and significant bearing on our future financial position."

The head of the family, Jorge, was so taken aback by Santiago's response that he sat, literally open-mouthed, looking startled. He quickly collected himself and gestured for Santiago to continue.

For the next 15 minutes or so, Santiago gave a review of the company's progress over the previous decade, highlighting the most important decisions that had led to its dramatic growth. He rattled off key metrics: capital invested, loans raised, cash flows, net profitability, return on investment. It was a very positive report; a business success story. But he also reminded them of the most difficult periods they had been through together.

"It wasn't all plain sailing; remember 2008 and the financial crash and the terrible uncertainty of those times?"

There were murmurs of agreement. The board remembered those difficult days very well.

"But, together, we pulled through. We weathered the worst of the storm. The decisions we made to put us back on the path to growth proved to be the right decisions. We are resilient and strong.

"Now, times are good again," Santiago continued. "But I believe we face a new challenge and a new danger. That danger is complacency. The world is changing rapidly. The pandemic and unforeseen wars in Europe and the Middle East have shown us how supply chains can be quickly disrupted. Nobody knows what the effects of

AI will be on our industry, but we know it will have a major impact. We need to change our corporate structure in ways that will make us more agile and more able to respond to the unexpected. The only thing we can be certain of, apart from death and taxes, is more uncertainty and change."

There was some muted laughter but also nods of agreement.

"Most important," Santiago continued, "we need further growth to ensure that we stay strong and resilient and are in robust financial health to face the next crisis, whenever it arrives. This is not the time to rest on our laurels. 'Steady as she goes' is actually a risky plan."

Santiago allowed himself a glance at his co-director, Jonathan.

"I would like to outline the strategy that I think will give us this increased agility and robustness. It involves substantial investment, and no investment comes without risks. But I am convinced the risk of carrying on with *business as usual* is far greater. On a more positive note, I am convinced that this new strategy and this new investment will produce dramatic growth, and that the wealth of the business will be greatly increased. This is a strategy that protects the company against future shocks by making us bigger, stronger and wealthier."

Santiago presented a series of slides outlining his plans for growth, a new corporate structure involving several senior new roles and, over time, a significant increase in the total workforce. He spelled out the investment required and outlined plans as to how this could be financed. He showed a number of charts forecasting the key new revenue streams and associated costs, and finished with a summary of the expected return on investment in five years' time. It was an impressive figure.

It was time for Santiago to make his central pitch to the board. He drew a deep breath and glanced at Jorge, the patriarch.

"I don't think I need to remind the board of the contributions I have made to the company over these last many years. In every one of the key decisions made in the past decade or more, I have been a key part of the decision-making process and the key driving force in implementing the chosen course of action. I am confident that I can deliver the strategy I have just outlined."

He paused. All eyes were fixed on him.

"But I can only implement the strategy if I am given sole control as CEO. I have the greatest respect for Jonathan" – he nodded in the direction of his co-director – "and I would like to retain his immensely valuable services as a consultant. His depth of experience is invaluable to us. But I cannot drive these changes in a committee of two. I must have executive control as CEO."

The room was silent.

"We all know each other very well," Santiago concluded. "You know me very well. I don't believe this is a decision that needs to be agonized over for very long. I am going to leave the room for however long you need to decide whether you accept my strategy… in outline, of course, because there is obviously a great deal of discussion still to be had about the detail. But, more importantly, whether you are prepared to appoint me as CEO to carry out the final version of this strategy we would all agree on. If you feel you're unable to offer me the role of CEO, I regret that I must offer my resignation."

He headed for the door. Jorge tried to call him back, but Santiago was adamant.

"I've given you a lot to think about," he said, in even tones. "It's best you talk, now, in private. I think I've given the board everything it needs to decide. I feel the organization must move forward, and I'm prepared to lead the charge, but I need to know that I am in control of that. I'm not prepared to carry on with the status quo. It's now or never."

He left the room.

The stunned silence continued until Jorge broke the ice, addressing the board.

"Well gentlemen, ladies. It seems we have a lot to talk about. Who would like to go first?"

Santiago took a seat in the waiting area anteroom outside the boardroom. An assistant offered him coffee, which he refused. She looked at him quizzically but quickly got the message and retreated to her desk, where she stared intently at her computer screen.

Santiago felt strangely calm. In fact, he felt happy. He smiled quietly to himself and picked up a magazine lying on a side table. He was quietly reading when Jorge himself opened the door.

"Could you join us again, Señor Martinez?" he asked. He was smiling broadly. As Santiago approached the door, Jorge held out his hand. As they shook hands, Jorge put his other arm around Santiago's shoulders and ushered him into the room.

"Come and talk to us. We have a lot to do."

Santiago was made CEO – of course – and his transformation strategy was accepted. His co-director, Jonathan, was quick to congratulate him. Santiago thanked him and reiterated the offer of a continuing consultancy role. "Let's get together and talk soon," he said, smiling.

I met Santiago a week or so later for our next coaching session. We had a lot to talk about, but my first question was obvious.

"How are you feeling?"

"I feel good!" he said, grinning. "But also, a bit foolish. What took me so long?"

"Emotion," I said. "You knew the logic of the situation, but your emotions were holding you back. The board saw you in one light, and that colored your own view of yourself, as did your history with the company.

"It's different when you come in at a senior level instead of working your way up through the ranks. You needed to use tactics to bring your emotions in line with the logic your brain was telling you was perfect: that you had the right vision and experience and were perfectly positioned to be the CEO of the company. The ultimatum to the board was the perfect tactic to link the logic to your own emotions and those of the board. It was like an ultimatum to them, but also to yourself. Well done!"

Santiago – or Señor Martinez as I would like to think of him now – smiled happily.

"Now," I said, "let's talk about this strategy. I like the look of it. Tell me about the pieces you feel least certain about."

Storytelling is at the heart of effective leadership. As the storytelling guru Geoff Mead articulates in his book, *Telling the Story: The Heart and Soul of Successful Leadership*, stories are not merely a way to communicate. They are the most potent means of connection, inspiration and alignment. They allow leaders to link logic, emotion and tactics in a cohesive and compelling way, making the abstract tangible and the complex relatable.

STORYTELLING: THE BRIDGE BETWEEN VISION AND ACTION

Mead's insights remind us that every leader, like every individual, is living their own story. Leadership, then, is not about dictating tasks or goals but about weaving a collective narrative that connects each team member's personal journey to the organization's shared vision. This aligns deeply with the central principle in author and inspirational speaker Simon Sinek's book, *Start with Why* – that the most effective leaders inspire by clarifying why their vision matters and how it resonates on a personal level with those they lead.

In businesses, this begins with understanding and articulating the foundational story: how the organization began, what values shaped it, and what struggles and triumphs have defined its journey. From there, leaders must craft a future-oriented narrative that invites participation, energizes action and creates alignment. As Mead emphasizes, every organization has built-in stories waiting to be told; stories that can unify teams and drive purpose.

CRAFTING STORIES FOR CONNECTION

Santiago's journey from intern to CEO exemplifies the transformative power of storytelling. For years, his inability to step into the chief executive role stemmed from an outdated narrative - one where he was still 'young Santi,' overshadowed by the story of the company's founding and his superiors' perceptions of him. His breakthrough came when he redefined his narrative, presenting himself as the hero ready to lead the organization into its next chapter.

This shift echoes Mead's principle; that a story is not just about recounting facts but about giving them meaning. Santiago's ultimatum - clear, logical and emotionally resonant - was not just a statement of intent, but a narrative device that galvanized the board to see him in a new light. It was also a moment of personal transformation, allowing him to align his actions with his belief in his capabilities.

THE ROLE OF HUMILITY IN STORYTELLING

Media strategist Ryan Holiday's book, *Ego is the Enemy*, offers a crucial counterpoint to the power of storytelling: the importance of humility. Leaders must be mindful that the story they tell is not about themselves but about the collective journey. Ego distorts narratives, turning them into self-serving monologues rather than inclusive dialogues. In Santiago's case, his success came not from emphasizing his importance, but demonstrating how his leadership aligned with the organization's best interests and the board's shared goals.

PERSONAL STORIES: BECOMING THE HERO

On a personal level, storytelling is equally powerful. As Mead and others suggest, the stories we tell ourselves shape our identities and behaviors. Too often, individuals like Santiago become trapped in limiting narratives – stories that emphasize inadequacy, failure or self-doubt. These stories, consciously or unconsciously, reinforce negative patterns and prevent growth.

The key to transformation lies in rewriting these narratives. Instead of seeing ourselves as constrained by past failures or external perceptions, we must create stories that celebrate resilience, learning and potential. Santiago's decision to envision himself as CEO, and then act on that vision, illustrates how a new narrative can unlock action and achievement.

CONNECTING STORIES TO L.E.T.

The L.E.T. framework is itself a storytelling model. It provides the structure for crafting narratives that inspire and drive action:

- **Logic:** The foundation of any story. In Santiago's case, the logic was clear: his past contributions to the company and the skills, capabilities and deep understanding of the company that placed him uniquely as the leader best able to drive future growth.
- **Emotion:** The driver of engagement. Santiago's confidence in presenting his strategy and his ultimatum was rooted in his emotional connection to the company's success and his belief in his own leadership abilities.
- **Tactics:** The path to realization. By aligning his strategy with actionable steps and presenting a clear plan to the board, Santiago bridged the gap between vision and execution.

LESSONS FOR LEADERS

1. **Understand the Power of Narrative**
   Leaders must continually craft and communicate the story of their organization, aligning it with their vision and the personal journeys of their team members.
2. **Start with Why**
   As Simon Sinek emphasizes, the *why* behind the story gives it meaning and inspires action. Without it, even the most compelling narrative will fall flat.

3. **Rewrite Limiting Stories**
   Personal growth begins with recognizing and reshaping the stories we tell ourselves. As leaders, we must also help others rewrite their narratives to unlock potential.

4. **Connect Emotion to Action**
   Stories must evoke emotion to drive behavior. By tying emotional resonance to logical plans and actionable steps, leaders can create momentum and engagement.

5. **Practice Humility**
   Effective storytelling is about service, not self-aggrandizement. Leaders must craft narratives that revolve around the collective, not the individual.

Storytelling is the thread that ties together the logical, emotional and tactical elements of leadership. It is the way we make sense of the past, envision the future and inspire action in the present. As Mead writes: "A great leader is not the star of the story but its narrator, helping others see their roles and inviting them to co-create the journey."

For leaders, the challenge is to continually refine their narrative, ensuring that it reflects their vision, connects with their audience and inspires meaningful action. Like Santiago, we must all find the courage to tell our stories with authenticity, purpose and heart. It is through these stories that we lead and live.

CHAPTER 15

THE PHOENIX

I think it's human to make mistakes. I think it's human to get confused. I think it's human to fail and to be weak at times. But I also think it's human to be resilient. I think it's also human to decide what kind of mindset you want to have. I think it's also human to motivate yourself and recognize and value who you are and what you have to offer. That's why you have to put your treasures into boxes. Boxes where you put the success you have had, the failures that you have had, how you became resilient and came through those challenges. Study each one of them. Look for solutions. Talk to people smarter than yourself. Look for answers in books, in movies, from friends and colleagues, and you will find yourself with more logical elements that will help you make good decisions and develop a strong mindset. Because the mindset will allow you to act tactically – to understand when the timing is right to do things and what action to take.

I remember my dad calling me a 'phoenix' many times throughout my life. To him, it was more than a nickname; it was a testament to my resilience, my ability to bounce back from the toughest blows and rise from every challenge. In my mind, this is how I interpreted his nickname for me.

Consider the myth of the phoenix, a magnificent bird that symbolizes rebirth and transformation. The phoenix lives for centuries, but when it feels its end approaching, it builds a nest and sets itself on fire. From the ashes, a new, young phoenix emerges, reborn and ready to begin its life anew. This cycle of death and rebirth is essential for the phoenix to attain its full strength and glory.

Humans also undergo cycles of vulnerability, weakness and transformation. Just as the phoenix must endure the flames to rise again, we must face our own challenges and periods of fragility. These experiences shape us, forging our strength and resilience.

Embrace your moments of struggle and transformation, because they are the fires that prepare you to rise stronger and more brilliant. Like the phoenix, your journey of continuous growth and renewal makes you formidable and extraordinary.

Reflecting on my own journey, I see how my father's metaphor of the phoenix became a guiding light. Every setback, every moment of vulnerability and every challenge was a necessary fire that I had to endure. These experiences were not merely obstacles; they were transformative flames that forged my character and resilience.

In the realm of business and leadership, embracing the phoenix within means recognizing that every failure and hardship is an opportunity for rebirth and growth. It's about understanding that the pressures and dark moments are not signs of weakness, but rather the essential forces that strengthen us.

When we encounter difficulties, we have two choices: to succumb to the flames or to rise from them. The process of transformation is not easy. It demands courage, patience and unwavering belief in our capacity to emerge stronger. Just as the phoenix knows its rebirth is inevitable, we must trust in our ability to overcome and evolve.

As you navigate your own path, remember that growth often comes from the most challenging experiences. Embrace your moments of fragility and transformation, because they are the crucible that prepares you for greater achievements. Like the phoenix, let your journey be one of continuous renewal and empowerment.

By embodying the spirit of the phoenix, we can approach change not with fear, but with the confidence that every ending is merely the beginning of a new chapter. We can rise from our ashes stronger and more brilliant, ready to face the world with renewed strength and vision.

Every challenge I faced taught me the art of resilience. Moments of doubt became stepping stones toward the confidence I now carry. I've fallen many times, but each fall gave me the strength to rise again and the wisdom to know that setbacks are temporary. Resilience isn't about standing tall without faltering, it's about knowing how to pick yourself up, again and again, with grace and determination.

Working across different cultures and industries taught me one valuable truth: authenticity, above all, is the key to leading with impact. I found in solitude a chance to reconnect, and in that quiet I learned that the best companion I can ever have is myself. Self-love became my foundation – it was never about being perfect, but about embracing my flaws and knowing that I am enough, just as I am.

I've extended a hand to many, but I learned the importance of boundaries and the patience to wait for others to be ready to accept help. Striving for excellence has shown me that imperfections are where growth happens. They push us to refine, to adapt, to improve.

I commit fully to what is necessary, and I respect the pace at which others move through their own journeys. Watching others rush to an undefined finish line taught me to cherish each step, knowing that lasting success is built on steady, intentional progress. In both business and life, nothing is promised, but that's what makes each moment valuable. The here and now is where life happens.

People come and go, and I've learned that their time in my life isn't something to control. Those who matter will stay because they choose to, showing their commitment through actions, not words. True connection, whether in friendship or life partnership, is rare and priceless. It is built on trust, understanding and mutual growth. I no longer seek validation from others; care and loyalty show themselves naturally when shared values and genuine love are at the core. Commitment is never an obligation; it is a privilege when driven by genuine passion and mutual respect.

Living fully means embracing every part of the journey – the highs, the lows, the growth that comes with every experience. I've learned to focus on my progress and to celebrate my growth, knowing that mistakes don't define me. They refine me.

Some wounds run deep, but resilience means finding the strength to heal, knowing that I am capable of moving forward. Self-love has taught me that my worth isn't defined by anyone else; it comes from within. It's in the way I care for myself, the way I show up for myself, every day.

And those special moments? They often arrive when I've stopped chasing them, when I've let go and trusted the process.

The best of life is already unfolding – my only task is to stay open, resilient and ready to receive it.

As we near the end of this book, I am struck by the profound power of the phoenix, the mythical creature that has become not only my father's symbol for me but also a guiding force throughout my life. The phoenix, with its cycles of death and rebirth, embodies resilience, transformation and renewal. It represents not only who I strive to be, but also the essence of what life demands of us: to rise from the ashes of our trials stronger, wiser and more luminous.

The stories we tell – about ourselves, about others, and about our journeys – are the lifeblood of our growth. These stories have shaped who I am today, providing guidance, inspiration and comfort during moments of darkness. They are the threads connecting my love for books, the lessons I've learned and the experiences that have defined me.

A LIFE SHAPED BY STORIES

Books have been my sanctuary, my guide and my constant companion. *The Alchemist* by the Brazilian novelist Paulo Coelho taught me to trust in the universe and the journey of self-discovery. Professional basketball player Kobe Bryant's *The Mamba Mentality: How I Play* instilled in me the discipline to embrace challenges with unwavering dedication. Psychologist and behavioral economist Daniel Kahneman's *Noise: A Flaw in Human Judgement* sharpened my understanding of human decision-making, while the novels of Carlos Ruiz Zafón and George R.R. Martin transported me to worlds where stories come alive, where heroes rise and fall and where every choice carries weight.

Poems by Edgar Allan Poe and Ralph Waldo Emerson have whispered truths about life's complexities and the beauty of the human spirit.

One of Emerson's most quoted reflections on success is not a traditional poem but a prose-like piece that captures his philosophy:

To laugh often and much;
To win the respect of intelligent people and the affection of children;
To earn the appreciation of honest critics and endure the betrayal of false friends;
To appreciate beauty;
To find the best in others;
To leave the world a bit better, whether by a healthy child, a garden patch, or a redeemed social condition;
To know even one life has breathed easier because you have lived.
This is to have succeeded.

And this short and haunting poem by Poe, 'Alone,' reflects on internal struggles, loneliness and the darker narratives within:

From childhood's hour I have not been
As others were—I have not seen
As others saw—I could not bring
My passions from a common spring.
From the same source I have not taken
My sorrow; I could not awaken
My heart to joy at the same tone;
And all I loved, I loved alone.
Then—in my childhood—in the dawn
Of a most stormy life—was drawn
From every depth of good and ill
The mystery which binds me still:
From the torrent, or the fountain,
From the red cliff of the mountain,
From the sun that round me rolled
In its autumn tint of gold,
From the lightning in the sky
As it passed me flying by,
From the thunder and the storm,
And the cloud that took the form

(When the rest of Heaven was blue)
Of a demon in my view.

Each of these works has left an indelible mark, offering words, phrases and ideas that pushed me beyond life's barriers. Stories from these and other authors, and from the many people I've met along the way, reminded me that, even in the darkest moments, there is light to be found, growth to be embraced and wisdom to be gained.

THE FIRES THAT FORGE US

Like the phoenix, I have faced many metaphorical fires. At 11, I fell through the ice into a frozen lake, and my parents had to pull me out. They thought I was gone.

Years later, a misdiagnosis of a brain stroke led me to the operating room, only to be saved by the sharp judgement of a surgeon. His colleague had misread my scan and persuaded himself I was suffering from an aneurism. They were about to open up my skull and start poking around when the more senior surgeon diagnosed a migraine and sent me home with painkillers.

In the Dominican Republic on a business trip, I got abducted by bad guys with a gun held to my head. Miraculously, because of some bad-guy reasoning I will never get to hear about, they let me go.

These brushes with death taught me that life is fragile but also resilient. They are reminders of how precious every moment is.

Emotionally, I have known the fire of losing my children and the draining weight of adversity. These were moments when I felt empty, like I had nothing left to give. But every time, I found a way to rise again. My father's phoenix became my beacon – a reminder that within me was the strength to transform and thrive.

The phoenix's story teaches us to embrace change, to see every ending as a beginning, and to view struggles as opportunities for growth.

In my own journey, I've learned to approach challenges with humility, knowing that resilience is not about never falling, but about always rising. I've learned that failures are not permanent but transformative, and that the demons, ghosts and shadows of our past must be faced, not feared.

Reading, reflecting and sharing have become tools for understanding myself and others. Books have taught me to listen deeply, to lead authentically, and to connect with the humanity in every person I meet. They've helped me find my own story and given me the courage to rewrite it when needed.

I want the message of the phoenix to come to you as a whisper in your ear – a quiet reminder that you, too, are capable of rising. Every fire you face, every trial you endure, is forging you into someone stronger, wiser and more extraordinary. Embrace your journey. Honor your story. Trust in your ability to overcome, to transform and to shine.

Let me leave you with a final poem – a reflection on the phoenix and on the journey of life:

From ashes I rise, anew, reborn,
Through fires endured, through nights forlorn.
The flames are my teacher, the trials my guide,
A life unyielding, with strength inside.

Each fall a lesson, each scar a tale,
Through storms unending, I set my sail.
Like the phoenix aloft, my wings unfurl,
To meet the dawn and embrace the world.

This is my journey. This is my story. And now, it's yours.

Fly high. Rise often. And never stop believing in the brilliance of your own light.

CLOSING THOUGHTS:

L.E.T. YOUR JOURNEY BEGIN

Leadership is not a destination; it is an ongoing journey of self-discovery, connection and impact. By embracing the principles of Logic, Emotion and Tactics, you can navigate complexity with clarity, inspire others with authenticity and create meaningful, lasting change.

Let your journey be one of purpose, resilience and transformation. Let your leadership leave a legacy.

L.E.T. PROFILE OF A LEADERSHIP MODEL

The L.E.T. framework presents leadership as a dynamic blend of Logic, Emotion and Tactics. Together, these elements define a comprehensive approach to leadership, addressing not only the practical demands of decision-making and action, but also the deeply human need for connection, resilience and adaptability. Below, each dimension is expanded on to deepen its relevance and application in a leadership role.

LOGIC: THE FOUNDATION OF RATIONAL LEADERSHIP

Logic provides the structure for informed decision-making, problem-solving and critical thinking. These are the intellectual tools leaders use to understand challenges, evaluate options and craft solutions that serve organizational goals.

1. PROBLEM SOLVING

- **Role in Leadership:** Leaders are constantly faced with complex challenges that require innovative and practical solutions. Problem-solving is about understanding root causes, identifying constraints and finding viable paths forward.
- **Key Practices:**
  - › Break problems into smaller, manageable components.
  - › Use root cause analysis tools, such as the '5 Whys' or fishbone diagrams.
  - › Involve diverse team perspectives to uncover blind spots.

2. CRITICAL THINKING

- **Role in Leadership:** Critical thinking ensures that leaders approach situations with clarity and objectivity, evaluating evidence and assumptions before drawing conclusions.
- **Key Practices:**
  - › Question assumptions and challenge the status quo.
  - › Weigh the pros and cons of potential actions.
  - › Use structured methods like SWOT (Strengths, Weaknesses, Opportunities, Threats) analysis for strategic insights.

3. DECISION-MAKING

- **Role in Leadership:** Decision-making is the culmination of logic in action. Leaders must not only analyze options but also have the courage to make timely decisions and stand by them.
- **Key Practices:**
  - › Prioritize decisions based on urgency and impact.
  - › Use data to inform, but not dictate, decisions – balance analytics with intuition.
  - › Evaluate outcomes to refine future decision-making processes.

EMOTION: THE HEART OF HUMAN-CENTRIC LEADERSHIP

Emotion forms the connective tissue of leadership, allowing leaders to inspire, support and build trust with their teams. It encompasses the leader's relationship with themselves and their ability to forge meaningful connections with others.

1. RESILIENCE

- **Role in Leadership:** Resilience enables leaders to navigate adversity with grace, maintaining focus and composure even during crises.
- **Key Practices:**
  - › Cultivate a growth mindset: view challenges as opportunities to learn.
  - › Practice emotional regulation to stay calm under pressure.
  - › Share personal stories of overcoming adversity to inspire others.

2. MOTIVATION

- **Role in Leadership:** Leaders must not only be motivated but also possess the ability to motivate others, aligning individual aspirations with organizational goals.
- **Key Practices:**
  - › Recognize and celebrate small wins to sustain morale.
  - › Set clear, meaningful goals that connect with team members' personal aspirations.
  - › Foster a culture of recognition and appreciation.

3. SELF-WORTH (KNOWING ONESELF)

- **Role in Leadership:** True leadership begins with self-awareness. Leaders must understand their strengths, weaknesses, values and triggers to lead authentically.
- **Key Practices:**
  - › Engage in regular self-reflection and seek feedback.
  - › Invest in personal development and mental wellbeing.
  - › Embrace vulnerability as a strength, not a weakness.

TACTICS: THE ENGINE OF EXECUTION

Tactics translate logic and emotion into action. They are the actionable strategies and behaviors that allow leaders to turn vision into reality.

1. STRATEGIC PLANNING

- **Role in Leadership:** Strategic planning provides the roadmap for achieving goals, outlining clear steps and allocating resources effectively.

- **Key Practices:**
  - Define SMART (Specific, Measurable, Achievable, Relevant, Time-bound) objectives.
  - Break long-term goals into short-term milestones.
  - Regularly review and adjust plans based on outcomes and feedback.

2. COMMUNICATION (STORYTELLING AND NARRATIVE)

- **Role in Leadership:** Communication is the glue that holds teams together. Storytelling and narrative give logic and emotion their human context, making plans relatable and inspiring.
- **Key Practices:**
  - Use storytelling to align teams around a shared vision.
  - Tailor communication styles to fit the audience, ensuring clarity and resonance.
  - Reinforce the organizational mission through repeated and consistent narratives.

3. ADAPTABILITY (AGILITY)

- **Role in Leadership:** Adaptability ensures leaders can pivot in response to changing circumstances without losing sight of their vision.
- **Key Practices:**
  - Stay informed about industry trends and emerging technologies.
  - Encourage a culture of innovation and experimentation.
  - Be open to feedback and ready to revise plans as needed.

THE L.E.T. LEADERSHIP ROLE: AN INTEGRATED APPROACH

A leader who masters the L.E.T. framework embodies these qualities:

1. **Logical Strategist**
   They craft clear, rational plans to address challenges and seize opportunities.

2. **Emotionally Intelligent Connector**
   They inspire trust, resilience and commitment through empathy and self-awareness.

3. **Tactical Executor**
   They turn ideas into impactful action, ensuring agility and alignment with organizational goals.

By integrating logic, emotion and tactics, leaders not only navigate the complexities of modern leadership but also create environments where teams can thrive. This triad provides the foundation for sustainable growth, innovation and collective success.

As I bring this book to a close, I find myself not at the end but at the threshold of a new beginning. This chapter may be complete, but my story continues to unfold, with new characters to meet, new challenges to face and new dreams to build. The most important 'new' characters I have been meeting are my children, now grown into adults. We stopped seeing each other because of the divorce, amid all the pain and difficulty that accompanied that, as with many divorces. Now we are getting to know each other all over again. The path ahead is one of change – an exhilarating mix of possibility and uncertainty. It is a journey that stirs both courage and vulnerability, as I step into uncharted territories and allow life to unfold in ways I cannot yet predict.

Through the lessons and stories I have shared with you, I hope you've discovered the threads that connect us all. The journey of navigating complexity with **Logic**, anchoring ourselves in **Emotion** and moving decisively with **Tactics** is both deeply personal and profoundly universal. Each phase of change – uncertainty, creativity and growth – requires us to draw on these elements in unique and powerful ways.

In moments of uncertainty, it is **Logic** that offers clarity and steadiness, much like the methodical genius of a detective assembling the pieces of a puzzle. Logic grounds us, helping us see the path ahead when the world feels chaotic. Yet, logic alone cannot carry us forward. We must also feel.

It is **Emotion** that breathes life into our plans, connecting us to one another and to our purpose. Like the quiet strength of a hero who balances raw humanity with unshakable resolve, emotion ignites the courage to be vulnerable, the warmth to empathize and the passion to dream. In the creative spark of emotion, we stop clinging to the past and instead see the beauty of what could be.

And then, there are the **Tactics**, the bridges between what we imagine and what we bring to life. Tactics remind us that success is not achieved in a single leap but in a series of deliberate, purposeful steps. They are the strategies that transform vision into reality, guiding us toward growth and grounding us in action.

These elements – Logic, Emotion and Tactics – have shaped not only the framework of this book but the foundation of my life. As I step into this new chapter, I carry the echoes of those who have inspired me: the logical mind that questions, the courageous heart that feels and the bold spirit that acts. The characters from my youth – Bruce Wayne, James Bond, Sherlock Holmes, Albert Einstein – are more than inspirations; they are reminders of the multifaceted strength we all possess when we allow ourselves to embrace complexity.

For you, the reader, I offer this: Embrace the transitions in your life with curiosity and grace. Feel the uncertainty without fear, let creativity stir within you, and trust that growth will follow. Use logic to find your footing, emotion to anchor your purpose and tactics to propel you forward. The journey may not always be easy, but it is in the fires of challenge that we are forged, like the phoenix rising anew, stronger and more luminous than before.

Let It Happen is not about passivity but about trust. Trust in yourself, trust in the process and trust in the unfolding of your unique story. It's about stepping into life's uncertainties with open arms, guided by the clarity of logic, the depth of emotion and the power of action.

As I move forward with my family, my work and my passions – guided by my Triumphometer, my emotions and, of course, my horses – I invite you to do the same. Together, let's rise, rebuild and let life unfold, with all its challenges and wonders.

The next chapter begins now.

L.E.T. it Happen.

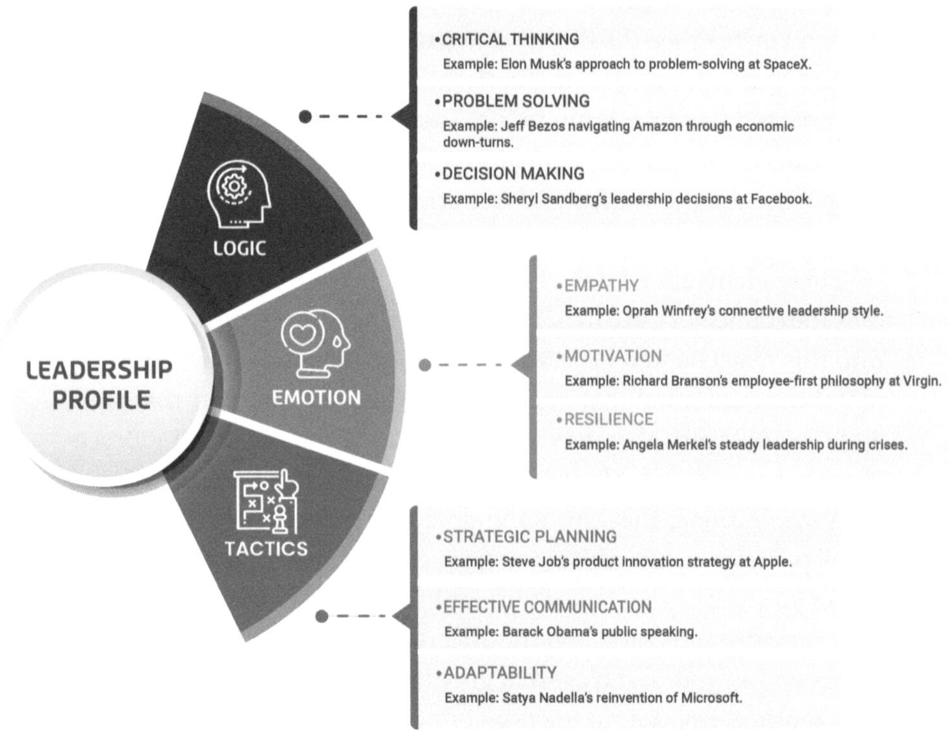

ACKNOWLEDGMENTS

This book is the result of different phases in my life – from growing up naive about life (not that I have stopped being naive, just a different kind of naive), and facing the challenges that life inevitably brings at a young age, to becoming a professional, a business owner, starting a family and experiencing collapse. Every story in this book is real. It contains my personal interpretation of how these events affected me, how I've channelled them and what I've learned. To all the characters in these stories – you know who you are – thank you for your vulnerability, for sharing your experiences and for allowing me to become a part of your narrative.

To all my mentors and teachers, some encountered formally and others informally around countless pints of beer, thank you. Many are no longer around, yet their teachings, advice and words remain indelibly imprinted on who I've become. Your knowledge, the challenges you posed – often unknowingly – and your willingness to allow disagreement were fundamental parts of my growth.

My family: My father, Nachito, whose presence continues powerfully despite his physical absence; my mother, Mayu, whose love and fascination with family keep our bonds strong; my siblings, who supported my journey away from Mexico and through life – I remain forever grateful. My children, Paige, Dany (Maury), Joseph and Emma, whose curiosity, love and determination inspire me daily; witnessing your journeys and stories enriches my own profoundly. Special thanks to Elizabeth – your support, insightful feedback on each chapter and care significantly improved this book; your love is embedded in every page.

Finally, to you, my reader – without you, this book is merely words on paper. Your act of reading, relating and extracting value from it transforms it into a true book, fulfilling its purpose.

Thank you,
Mau Espinosa

ABOUT THE AUTHOR

Mauricio Espinosa, fondly known as Coach Mau, is an inspiring entrepreneur, internationally renowned speaker and expert in leadership and transformational change. As the founder and president of G20, Inc., Mau has been a transformative force in the global automotive industry for nearly three decades, driving growth and innovation across North America, Europe, Asia and Latin America.

Mau's L.E.T. system is a groundbreaking exploration of leadership that merges logic, emotion and tactics into a powerful philosophy for personal and professional change. He is also a contributor to the influential book Roadmap to Success, sharing insights alongside legendary figures Dr Deepak Chopra and Dr Ken Blanchard.

Mau holds a Master's degree in Leadership and Coaching for Change from Oxford University's Saïd Business School and HEC Paris, and has specialized training from Harvard Law School in negotiation strategies. His career has been marked by developing revolutionary methods such as the P.E.P.R. business model (Productivity, Efficiency, Profitability and Returns) and the acclaimed L.E.T. leadership framework.

Born and raised in Mexico, Mau now calls Kansas City home. When not transforming businesses, he enjoys spending quality time with his children, family, and friends, embracing life's simple pleasures – riding horses, dancing (enthusiastically, though not always gracefully), playing golf and hitting the gym. He loves attending concerts, savoring fine cuisine paired with great wine, and never misses the opportunity to enjoy a perfectly poured Guinness.

Mau's passion and authenticity resonate deeply with audiences worldwide, from executive boardrooms to international conferences. His engaging approach and unwavering dedication have empowered thousands of individuals and organizations – including Audi, Volkswagen, Nissan, General Motors, Toyota and Scotiabank – to achieve extraordinary results.

Through his continuing journey as a thought leader and coach, Mau remains committed to unlocking human potential, challenging conventional wisdom and inspiring meaningful, lasting change.